FIGHTING FOR
CANADA

FIGHTING FOR
CANADA

Diane Francis

KEY PORTER BOOKS

Canadian Cataloguing in Publication Data

Francis, Diane, 1946–

        Fighting for Canada

ISBN 1-55013-796-4

1. Canada – Politics and government – 1993– .
2. Quebec (Province) – History – Autonomy and
independence movements. I. Title.

FC635.F73 1996   971.064′8   C96-930896-5

F1034.2.F73   1996

The publisher gratefully acknowledges the assistance of the Canada Council and the Ontario Arts Council.

Key Porter Books
70 The Esplanade
Toronto, Ontario
Canada M5E 1R2

Printed and bound in Canada

96 97 98 99 5 4 3 2 1

Contents

Acknowledgements

This book would not have been possible without the help of others. My researcher, Andrew Male, and executive assistant, Barbara Maxwell, have contributed enormously to this project. I would also like to thank publishers Anna Porter and Susan Renouf for their patience and belief in the outcome. Editor Geoffrey Huck and columnist William Johnson strengthened the manuscript immeasurably with their knowledge of Quebec politics and history.

Introduction

Like most English Canadians, I have been frightened away from Quebec politics because I'm told the issues are complicated, rooted in history, subtle, and comprehensible only to persons who speak and understand French. So I have deferred to successive Quebec-born prime ministers to sort it all out. But three decades and three Quebec prime ministers later, on October 30, 1995, we nearly lost Canada as we know it. And for no good reason.

We were just 52,000 votes away from being plunged into an economic and political crisis that was unimaginable. The currency would have collapsed and the Americans would have faced the prospect of another Mexico-style bailout. This was because Canadian governments owed more money to foreigners, mostly Americans, than any other nation on earth. These investors would have found the value of their holdings disappearing, which could have had repercussions on the value of the American dollar. Americans had huge investments inside Canada too and Canada is the United States's biggest customer and supplier.

In many ways, this book began where the country nearly ended. After that referendum, I began devoting myself to finding out what has really been going on in Quebec. I have concluded that Canadians are the victims of a conspiracy of separatists. More importantly, I have come to the realization that what these three Quebec prime ministers and their political parties have allowed to occur during the past thirty years represents the biggest scandal in Canadian history.

Canadians have been victims of a dangerous squabble between members of Quebec's political elite. They have turned Ottawa into a debating society between francophones and have wasted the government's time and money needlessly. Even worse than the excessive amount of tax dollars spent by Quebec politicians to fuel this fratricidal nonsense is the loss of national pride. Everyone around the world knows about Quebec separatism, and since October 30 most have assumed that a divorce is inevitable.

Ironically, Quebecers—both anglophone and francophone—have been the biggest victims in all of this. Quebec's economy is a mess and its people are handcuffed to a system that impedes their ability to compete in the world or get along with their trading partners and fellow citizens.

Few Quebecers are committed to an ideology of separatism. There has never been a groundswell of popular support for independence among francophones in Quebec. The separatist ideology has been kept alive artificially, through the cunning, tricks and blunders of Quebec politicians on both sides of the issue. They have been aided and abetted in this disservice to the country by Canada's second-rate media.

This book records travels, experiences, conversations, and research. It introduces an unlikely cast of Canadian heroes who have never given up the fight for Canada. It also profiles enemies of this country, such as Jacques Parizeau and Lucien Bouchard.

The material in this book exposes what this country is

really up against. And the problem rests as much with Ottawa as with Quebec City. Until Canadians understand this and demand change, the culprits will continue to run amok until they destroy the morale and economy of this country.

Canada should not be taken for granted. It is perhaps the finest country on the planet. But only if Canadians are willing to fight for it.

1
The Separatist Seduction

I first met Jacques Parizeau in 1985 while working on my book *Controlling Interest: Who Owns Canada?* He had resigned in November 1984 as Quebec minister of finance because his Parti Québécois had finally placed separatism on the back burner, years after its rejection by Quebecers in the 1980 referendum.

Even though he was out of the so-called loop, I had felt an interview was important. That's because he was one of the principal architects of the complex of nationalist policies and public enterprises, nicknamed "Quebec Inc." by the media, that had benefited a generation of francophones. My book was about the dangers of concentration of economic power, and Parizeau had played a key role in counteracting concentration with his "Quebec Inc." policies. So had other provincial governments. But few had done so much so quickly.

Parizeau agreed with the book's thesis. It was on his wave length. He had become an aggressive combatant against corporate growth for two reasons. He was an ardent socialist who disliked capitalists; but he was also an ardent Quebec nationalist who disliked anglophone Quebecers. And the fact that so much of Quebec's concentration of economic power was in the hands of anglos made the rich an even juicier target for him. So he made it his business to drive out or replace anglophone enterprises or reduce their importance. It was never billed as being that blatant, but that's what it was: corporate ethnic cleansing.

A *Toronto Star* colleague, Quebec City bureau chief Bob Mackenzie, knew where to reach Parizeau, who agreed to meet immediately, and said he liked the *Toronto Star* because Mackenzie had always dealt fairly with him and his party. The *Star* was left wing, as was Parizeau, and Mackenzie's wife was a high-ranking francophone Quebec City civil servant.

Parizeau and René Lévesque had been the chain-smoking odd couple of separatism. Parizeau was the brains and Lévesque the personality. Parizeau dressed like a British banker. Lévesque looked like an unmade bed. Parizeau was a brilliant egghead, Lévesque street smart.

Of the two, Parizeau was the more relaxed. He played around with interviewers and performed at the drop of a hat. He was a journalist's delight because he was both articulate and quotable.

My interview with him took place in his office in Montreal. After leaving the Parti Québécois he had become an academic, and was teaching at the business faculty of a university, the Haute Études Commerciales. This career suited him better than did politics, in many ways. He had trained to be an academic, earning a Ph.D. in economics from the London School of Economics and post-secondary degrees from universities in Paris. He was a thinker, not a glad-handing crowd-pleaser.

But burrowed away in academia he was out of the limelight, and he clearly missed it. After all, he had gone from being a powerful finance minister with a car and driver and fancy offices to the lowly status of an academic with one secretary and a sparsely furnished office. The room was institutional and dreary, without colour or memorabilia. It looked as if it were borrowed or temporary.

It was a sunny day, but his blinds were partially drawn. He sat at his desk and puffed on cigarettes the whole time. Smoke curled and swirled visibly in the slats of sunshine that shone through the blinds. The chair was uncomfortable, but the interview was fascinating.

In 1984 separatism looked to be dead in the water. But the cunning Parizeau was just biding his time for a comeback. When asked why he had not given up, he said, "Because we will always be a pain in the neck, that's why we must separate. It's inevitable and cannot be reversed."

That first interview lasted two hours. He brilliantly and succinctly summarized the economic history of Upper and Lower Canada, then explained the types of policies he had helped devise to counteract negative trends. His spin was biased, but telling. Ontario had been unfairly given the steel plants, he said, which meant it got the auto jobs and other advantages while Quebec had lost out. But there were other problems afflicting Quebec's once pre-eminent economy, problems that had nothing to do with favouritism. The opening of the St. Lawrence Seaway had allowed inland ports to compete with Montreal's, thus removing its role as the country's most important port of entry and exit. The postwar shift in trade to the United States from Britain had removed even more shipping activity.

Parizeau spoke with precision, humour, and charm. He communicated more effectively than anyone I had ever interviewed. The root of this talent lay in his clear thinking and his thorough consistency: A leads to B, to C, to D, and so on.

But his brilliance also had to do with the rigours of his education. He gave one example: a doctoral-level oral examination on philosophy before a tribunal. He was given a theme: the single word "Dieu" or "God," and he had to expound on that topic for three hours without interruption. Similarly, a television producer friend had just videotaped Parizeau for a ten-part series on Quebec's economic history. Without notes or direction, my friend said, Parizeau delivered ten half-hour segments that were compelling.

Parizeau's intellectual virtuosity was not unusual among Quebec politicians. Former prime minister Pierre Trudeau and others were Jesuit-educated and brilliant rhetoricians and thinkers. The Jesuits trained leaders by teaching them the arts and classics, not commerce. They encouraged the best and brightest in Quebec to go into politics, the priesthood, or the professions. By contrast, English Canada's politicians have mostly been boring and intellectually second-rate. The best and brightest among English Canadians go into business or the professions.

The contrast between the political classes inside and outside Quebec is remarkably similar to the contrast between the political cultures of France and the United States. In France the most brilliant Jesuit-trained intellectuals are handpicked for government and become its presidents and prime ministers, because the French believe in the need for a well-trained elite to run the country's affairs, whereas in the United States and Canada the English-speaking culture trains its best and brightest to aim for wealth or the professions. This is because the English-speaking countries believe that their democratic, constitutionally driven political systems can run themselves, without the ministrations of a mandarin class.

These cultural differences have resulted in the relative superiority of Quebec's political class over English Canada's, and that superiority is possibly the biggest reason why Quebec issues, and Quebec politicians, dominate federal politics. It's not because Quebec issues deserve to dominate. It is a matter of asymmetrical aptitude when it comes to politics.

Parizeau was obviously a French-style elitist. After all, at the time of my interview with him he was out of power, but not willing to follow his party and take no for an answer from Quebecers after the 1980 referendum rejection. Parizeau knew better, because he was a ranking member of the elite, and he and the other separatist elitists believed they knew exactly what was good for Quebec. To many Canadians, including Quebecers, this arrogance smacks of a disdain for democracy.

Controlling Interest came out in the fall of 1986, with a substantial portion based on the Parizeau interviews. Not only had he and others reduced the concentration of anglo and American economic power in Quebec, but his crowning achievement was when he and former premier Jean Lesage convinced Ottawa that the province should be given control of its portion of the Canada Pension Plan, now known as the Caisse de Dépôt et Placements du Quebec.

This gave Quebec significant economic leverage, because the Caisse became the country's largest pool of capital and the country's biggest stock-market investor. The provincial government also gained clout in corporate boardrooms, because now a generation of Quebec politicians could reward or punish entrepreneurs and enterprises for political ends. The Caisse forced stockbrokers who dealt with it to make trades on the Montreal Stock Exchange, and put pressure on the managements of the Quebec-based companies to perform in a way that benefited Quebec. Run by political appointees, the Caisse was not just a nest egg for Quebecers: it was now an instrument to promote nationalism.

Moreover, Parizeau had been instrumental in helping bolster the Caisses Populaires, or credit unions. These small financial institutions had been around for decades, sprouting out of local Catholic Church parishes. He helped engineer a restructuring that improved their management and made them more powerful. By the 1980s the Caisses were far bigger than the six biggest chartered banks in terms of mortgage lending.

Other innovations included tax laws favouring investment in Quebec companies as well as aggressive subsidies to businesses. Non-Quebec entities, on the other hand, were pushed around. He manoeuvred two American giants, General Dynamics and International Paper, into selling their Quebec assets to Quebecers. These were all brilliant strategies to an economic nationalist like Parizeau. But they were also interventionist, unnecessary, and unfair.

In the fall of 1986 I toured the country to promote sales of *Controlling Interest*. Before going to Montreal, I called Parizeau to arrange to give him an autographed copy as a way of thanking him for all his help. He suggested dinner at the posh Ritz-Carlton Hotel dining room to celebrate my success. It was great fun and he entertained me for hours over caviar, champagne, and many other courses.

He was extremely attractive, a bon vivant and an engaging raconteur. He talked about his educational experiences and his extracurricular activities in Central European politics. His wife at the time, the late Polish-born novelist and intellectual Alicja Poznanska, had spent years secretly advising Poland's Lech Walesa and his Solidarity movement. Parizeau said Walesa and other Poles were frequent guests at their Montreal home. He said they talked of revolution over the kitchen table.

While helping Poles to stand up to the Russians and the Communists may have been admirable, Parizeau's involvement allowed him to hone his skills as a cunning, patient, and fearless revolutionary. And Canada was his opponent, just as Russia was for the Poles he advised.

Parizeau also talked about his family. His father had been a successful general insurance agent in Montreal. Both he and his brother, Robert, went to the best private schools. Jacques went on to become an academic while Robert went into the family business and eventually became one of the country's most successful commercial insurance broker/ agents, with privileges in Lloyd's of London. "We have some very interesting family discussions," he told me. "I'm a separatist and those two chaps are not. But my father has a strict rule. No politics at the dinner table."

Parizeau was unusual for a separatist; he had had the best of everything, a prosperous family and great prospects. Some speculated that after years of advising Liberals in

Quebec he became a separatist because the Liberals in Ottawa did not appoint him Governor of the Bank of Canada.

But he gave another explanation over dinner. After graduating from university in Montreal he went to Britain and France for a few years, to do postgraduate work. He attended the Institut d'Études Politiques et Études Supérieures de Sciences Économiques in Paris. After completing his studies, he decided to see the rest of his country and took a train trip westward in 1967 across Canada. He set off, a proud young man with a Ph.D. and a wealth of sophisticated knowledge and experience.

There were "incidents," he told me, without going into detail. He hinted at confrontations with bigots, the kind of nasty experience that still occasionally occurs: name-calling by anti-French bigots, who are mostly pathetic little people attempting to elevate their own low self-esteem by stereotyping ethnic minorities. All Parizeau said was that the trip convinced him that French Canadians would never be accepted in English Canada, and that independence was therefore the only option.

We stayed in touch. Months after our dinner, he helped me locate a French-language publisher for my book. In the spring of 1987 *Le Monopole* came out in Quebec in paperback. He also participated, as I did, in a conference in Montreal on concentration of economic power. He never hesitated to praise *Controlling Interest* or my efforts. He gave me access and was always on the other end of a telephone for an interview, never missing an opportunity to tell English Canada about the deep-seated grievances and injustices that had been visited upon francophones. His theology was seductive and unrelenting. And while he has been written off as arrogant and pompous by many, his persuasiveness and manipulative mind have been greatly underestimated by his foes.

The next interview was years later, in November 1990, just four months after the death of the proposed Meech Lake Accord. He was PQ leader now, and riding high in the polls due to the negative post-Meech publicity. Lucien Bouchard had bolted from the Tories and started the federal version of the PQ, the Bloc Québécois. Prime Minister Brian Mulroney was disdained in his home province and separatism was again alive and well and living in Quebec. Another referendum was inevitable and Parizeau's theology, in tatters in the mid-1980s, was in the ascendent.

As the situation for the nation worsened, I leaped at the chance to interview the reclusive anti-separatist tycoon Charles Bronfman, co-chairman of the gigantic distillery the Seagram Company. Bronfman did not want to talk about Quebec. He had only granted the interview to help promote the sale in Canada of Israel bonds. He was chairman of the fund-raising effort that year and his organization had approached me to write a piece supporting bond sales for a special advertising supplement in my newspaper, the *Financial Post*. The deal was that I would write a lead essay encouraging investment in the bonds in return for an interview with Bronfman.

A date was set and luckily Parizeau agreed to an interview that same day. My plan was to get Bronfman to talk about the separatists' popularity and perhaps about whether he would go or stay if they won an election. He had threatened to move Seagram's head office out of Quebec back in 1976, before René Lévesque won his first provincial election. His pledge had caused a furore, and many believed it affected the outcome of the referendum. As things turned out, Lévesque won, but Bronfman did not move out. I was interested to know whether Bronfman would make the same threat again. If Bronfman obliged I would ask Parizeau to react to it.

Bronfman's office was decorated with baseball mementoes from the time he owned the Montreal Expos. There was the famous picture of him in an Expos uniform, with autographed bats and balls and various trophies. A shy, retiring billionaire, he had remained in Montreal despite his threat. The reality was that Seagram had years before moved its real head office to New York City. That's where

Charles's brother, Edgar, ran the empire. Meanwhile, Charles was co-chairman but spent most of his time investing, giving money away to charitable causes, running his baseball team, and helping finance the Liberals.

The Bronfman interview was brief and was mostly about Israel's bonds. But as I expected, he repeated his threat to pull his stakes out of Quebec if the separatists won the next referendum on separation.

Happy to have snared a controversial quote, I walked the four blocks to Parizeau's office. He also reacted as I had expected. "Bronfman said that before. Those who wanted to leave have left," said a clearly peeved Parizeau, adding, "Poor old Charlie."

It was late, around 5:30 p.m., and Parizeau looked tired. He had just lost his wife of many years to a lengthy and lingering battle against cancer. When Alice was mentioned, tears welled up in his eyes.

He was as candid as usual but cockier than he had been before. The mood in Quebec was ugly, and a referendum on separation would have handily won, according to polls. This reversal had taken place because negative feelings towards the rest of Canada had been astutely whipped up by Parizeau and Quebec's separatist press. They billed the death of Meech Lake as English Canada's rejection of French language and culture. From my perspective, that was bunk. English Canada had signed on and only two provincial premiers, Gary Filmon of Manitoba and Clyde Wells of Newfoundland, caused its demise.

Parizeau out of power was charming, but as leader of the opposition Parti Québécois, which was enjoying unprecedented popular support, he was frightening. He stated for the first time that a separate Quebec would agree to assume only 17 percent of the federal debt, even though it represented 24 percent of the population. He said that, like it or not, Quebec would use Canadian currency and demand seats on the Bank of Canada's board of governors. He threatened that if Canada did not like those terms and others, Quebec might simply disrupt traffic on the St. Lawrence Seaway. He said that Quebec would demand to be a third-party signatory of every treaty or free trade agreement that Canada had signed. Or else. This was important, because Canada had negotiated a veto over new entrants to its U.S. or Mexico free trade agreements, providing Ottawa with a major bargaining chip if Quebec separatists ever obtained a mandate from voters to leave.

"What we want is everything to have a third, Quebec signature. What if the Americans don't want a third signature and push Quebec out of the Free Trade Agreement? Then Quebec must have the right to look at each treaty signed in our name. NORAD, the St. Lawrence Seaway, and dozens more. Either Quebec countersigns all these treaties in one afternoon, or we renegotiate them one by one. It'll be one incredible mess."

Besides such threats, he said Quebec had to leave because of egregious past events, not merely because it was a "pain in the neck" as he had said previously. He told me, for example, that francophone geologists were unable to find jobs in Canada until the 1970s. He agreed that wasn't the case any longer. He also agreed that any ambitious Quebecer should, like himself, speak English. "Yes," he said, surprisingly, and on the record, "and I'd like them to speak a third language, too."

In his mind, another justification for leaving was that Quebecers could only trust their own provincial government in Quebec City. "No one says that what was done at the federal civil service [in terms of bilingualism] was puny or ridiculous. But more often than not, when our own [Quebec] government opened the doors, intense conflict resulted on the so-called language front [with English-Canadians]. Language rights would not have been given to us. Doors were opened only by the Quebec government. Federal bilingualism came too late. We're not mad, and we understand full well you don't operate in international markets without English."

The interview was interesting as always; but he was different this time, threatening and talking about reneging on obligations such as debts. He also openly admitted the hypocrisy of imposing French-only policies on francophones in Quebec while at the same time agreeing that a knowledge of the English language was imperative in the new economic reality.

A month after these interviews ran in *Maclean's* magazine, I published another article in the *Post* underscoring how separation would be economic suicide. Quebec was too dependent upon imports, energy and non-energy, to service its debts and thrive on its own. English Canada would be upset and vindictive if Quebec reneged on its debts, and might refuse to let Quebec into the North American Free Trade Agreement with the United States and Mexico.

At that time Quebec City's *Le Soleil* bought and translated my weekend *Post* pieces. But that column was to be my last for *Le Soleil*. It was greatly criticized in the francophone press and I was fired.

My interview with Parizeau reinforced my fears about the fanaticism of the separatists. Parizeau was throwing around threats that could result in armed conflict, such as his threat to disrupt seaway traffic or renege on debts. He was dedicated to creating another crisis, no matter what effect it had on Canadians. That was the last time I spoke with Jacques Parizeau. Or wanted to.

2
Crime and Punishment

In June 1991, I became editor of the *Financial Post*, a job that entitles the lucky recipient to full-fledged membership in the Canadian establishment. My enhanced status became immediately apparent. Within days of the appointment, the quality of invitations jumped considerably. Suddenly, I was a desired dinner guest in some of the most rarefied salons in Canada, finding myself seated at the head table at important functions. Invitations to 24 Sussex, Rideau Hall, and the Royal Yacht Britannia came; access to the rich and powerful was assured; universities wanted lectures. The editor's pen was not just mightier than the sword. It was perceived to be a battalion.

But there was a price to pay for becoming part of the Canadian establishment. In some ways, Canada is like a small town afflicted with elites that exert enormous and dangerous social, and sometimes economic, control.

It was one year after the demise of Meech Lake and six months after I was fired by *Le Soleil* over the Parizeau interview. The prospects for unity looked grimmer than ever to

me as Lucien Bouchard and Jacques Parizeau alike continued to gain support for outright separation, according to
polls. As editor I felt that my columns, and the editorial policy of the newspaper, would have to pay attention to a
looming unity crisis. Separatists were damaging Canadian
business interests as well as the economy in general, and a
business newspaper such as the *Post* had to weigh in with
the business viewpoint. Clearly the paper was pro-unity and
in favour of the quickest, most painless resolution possible to
remove the cloud hanging over the country's economy.

I decided to do a series of interviews on unity and other
issues with the national political leaders, including Prime
Minister Brian Mulroney, Liberal opposition leader Jean
Chrétien, New Democrat leader Audrey McLaughlin, and
Bloc Québécois leader Lucien Bouchard.

Mulroney bemoaned the death of Meech Lake and
talked about the necessity of Quebec signing a new constitutional deal. McLaughlin said the same thing and Chrétien,
who opposed Meech, was vague as to what to do, as usual.

Mulroney was also clearly upset at Bouchard for leaving, even though he knowingly used separatist help in
Quebec to get elected in 1984 and again in 1988. The quid
pro quo was that Mulroney would come up with an acceptable new constitutional deal. Meech unravelled and
Bouchard bolted, forming the Bloc with a handful of other
Quebec Tories and Liberals.

Bouchard was hard to nail down, but a date in November
was chosen. There was a snow storm in Ottawa and my
flight arrived late. Once in the Parliament Buildings, I got
lost finding Bouchard's Bloc Québécois offices because they
were buried in the back of the building.

His office was dark and unkempt, as most parliamentarians' offices are. The buildings are depressing inside. Even
on sunny days, lamps are turned on. Bouchard was eating a
sandwich at his desk and was interrupted constantly by the
telephone. He was squeezing the interview in during his
lunch hour. There were none of the normal niceties or

small talk. He was not flirtatious or fun-loving like Parizeau. Intense and humourless, this man was no lady-killer despite the reputation. More mad monk than macho, he had eyes that were Lutheran and a voice that was monotone but very controlled.

He seemed depressed in these surroundings. Shortly after lending himself to the Mulroney cause, he had been given the ultimate francophone patronage plum, the ambassadorship to France. There he had lived like a king, courting a young American stewardess and entertaining lavishly before returning to a high-profile position back in Canada as an influential cabinet minister.

Now here he was, a mere member of Parliament in what appeared to be shared digs. His office was large, roughly twenty by forty feet in size, but cramped. Other desks were there, occupied by others. Looking back now on the interview, I see that he was amazingly prescient; on that day in 1991 he predicted the outcome of the next federal election, which was to take place in October 1993.

"The Reform Party will have fifty to sixty seats like us," he said. "The Tories will almost disappear without one seat in Quebec. Recent polls show the first seat to go will be the prime minister's. Tories will get nothing in the West. The Maritimes will go Liberal, Ontario will be open hunting. The NDP will be strong in B.C. and elsewhere. There will be Liberal and NDP seats in Ontario. Liberals will get some seats in Quebec.

"The Liberals will join the NDP and this is why it is so necessary for Quebec that the Bloc exists. We need to be strong there. The goal will not be to destroy a negotiation, but to disrupt it. As for the Reform Party, Preston Manning, I respect his political and economic culture. He represents something real and would be a very tough negotiator. He's a man of his time."

I suggested that "distinct society" was a language issue in Quebec but a civil rights one outside because the sign bylaw restricted language rights. "You are right, partly," he replied.

"People felt the bylaw was a breach of the Canadian model. English Canada's vision cannot abide the distinct society clause. Quebec needs it. During Meech Lake I saw Mulroney pressured by the rest to change or dilute it. I fought against him. I saw Mulroney drifting toward English Canada's requirements and the kind of terrible compromises that kill a country. Too grey, too equivocal, so I quit. I couldn't sell it. I felt betrayed. I was not intending to create a party or go on with politics."

What about civil rights in Quebec?

"We must work on this. I don't like it personally. Many people are like me and express an uneasiness about those laws. But if you reopen Bill 101, you must strengthen other controls. In a sovereign Quebec, there would be no hesitation to get rid of the prohibition on English signs. But we must protect the language of the majority, and the use of French in the workplace is a concern.

"There should be improvements in protection like a lower floor [the threshold in terms of the number of employees that triggers the requirement that the working language of firms must be French]. At the same time, there should be more guarantees to the English that their institutions will remain bilingual. This being said, I think we should also speak English. We must master English to do business. I will insist that my children speak perfect French and perfect English."

He dismissed economic concerns. I asked him why anyone would invest in Canada with such a cloud hanging over it?

"I understand that they might ask questions about the current situation. One of our main objectives is to extract a decision from the process. As of now it is difficult to convince anyone it's a marvellous place to invest. It is impossible to reconcile the two visions of the country. Everything will be decided in 1992 but in the meantime [investors should] not worry whether Quebec is in or out. We have responsible leaders and governments and hardworking people. The assessment agencies are not that worried."

I asked him about Parizeau's statement to me the year before that a separate Quebec would assume only 17 percent of the federal debt.

"I will not get into the figures. We will have to negotiate. It will be complex. Quebec will negotiate strongly. I know it is very dangerous, delicate. English-speaking Canadians believe Bourassa when he says there will be a deal, Quebec will cave in. You're wrong. You should get ready for that. Both [sides] have a common duty to retain the confidence of the international creditors. [As for] issuing our own currency, there will be a terrible effect of dumping all [Canadian] currency onto the market. We will work it out."

What about the aboriginal lands?

"It boils down to a legal question over the St. Lawrence Gulf and Arctic Islands. For the rest, we think we are on safe legal ground to keep territories as it stands now. Quebec will be very firm on this. We have been there for four hundred years and have a right to be there."

He obviously disliked his federal foe.

"Chrétien has no clout in Quebec. He's considered an Uncle Tom and is identified with the 1981–82 repatriation of the Constitution. He's the kind of Quebecer who never should be in Ottawa. I could never make a deal with Chrétien. Never. Never. My dislike for him is visceral, not reconcilable. We will not be here to make deals. We will make sure during this critical time the federal negotiators are dealing straight with Quebec and not waging economic war. We will form tactical alliances around specific laws but no general alliance with anyone. We will never be part of this country."

What was most disturbing about Bouchard was his refusal to admit that separation meant economic hardship. "There's no evidence living standards would be much lower. If Quebec says yes, separation won't happen the next day. There will be a one-year delay and the debt will be financed as usual. We must accept that English Canada doesn't want to look at it [the possibility of separation]. The English are ostriches. We'd need time for the shock to recede."

I asked him about controversial remarks Pierre Trudeau had just made that an independent Quebec would deport anglos because separatists were racist?

"What bugs me is he thought he was protected by being off the record and he spoke from his heart. He thought he was with family. It was terrible. I have some sense of history, deportation. It happened once with the Acadians, done by the British. Why [did Trudeau say it]? Because Trudeau despises his people. Trudeau never accepted to be born a French Canadian. It tells much more about Trudeau than about Quebec. He doesn't like them, despises them. Look at how he signed the Constitution [in 1982] without Quebec there."

The interview raised even more disturbing questions. Parizeau's new attitude was worrisome, but he was never going to be the box-office favourite that Lévesque had been. After all, he was arrogant and pompous, parading around in waistcoats spouting anglophile colloquialisms such as "chaps" and "bloody." He was not a man of the people. Some francophone commentators made fun of his anglophile affectations.

Bouchard was different. Unlike Parizeau, he was a potentially popular ideologue, the most dangerous type of political opponent. This was not a man who would accommodate compromise. This was a man who could inflame an audience because of his deep-rooted and emotional beliefs. He had sacrificed a great deal for the cause, unlike the bon-vivant Parizeau.

Even worse, Bouchard was totally blind about economic consequences while Parizeau at least paid lip service to them. The two were also planning to embark on a new, more dangerous strategy. The next referendum was not going to be about some vague concept known as sovereignty-association. It was going to be about outright secession after a Yes vote and a subsequent unilateral declaration of independence.

By just leaving, separatists would force English Canada

to capitulate or take up arms. This was unlikely, given the cowardly behaviour of past prime ministers. "English Canadians will be reasonable," Parizeau crowed.

But unilateral declarations of independence are illegal in most countries, including Canada. Several constitutional law experts, including Professor Stephen Scott of McGill University and York University's Peter Hogg, had written that the borders of this country could never be altered by political negotiation behind closed doors or by a Yes vote in a provincial referendum. The borders could only change as a result of an amendment to the constitution, which would require the consent of seven provincial legislatures with at least 50 percent of the population as well as the consent of the House of Commons. Any attempt by Quebec to change the borders of Canada or leave the country unilaterally by political edict would be unconstitutional.

This legal question was successfully tested during the last Quebec referendum, in October 1995, when Guy Bertrand, a Quebec City lawyer and an ex-separatist, won a decision from the Quebec Superior Court that the separatists' planned unilateral declaration of independence contravened constitutional protections for residents of Quebec. After the referendum, Bertrand began the process of taking the matter all the way to the Supreme Court of Canada to establish a precedent. As former constitutional law adviser to the separatist leader René Lévesque during the 1980 referendum and subsequent constitutional talks with the government of Pierre Trudeau, Bertrand had researched the subject.

"A group of us had suggested to Lévesque that we just unilaterally secede and see what Canada does, but Lévesque said, 'That is illegal, and we are democrats,'" recalled Bertrand in an interview with me a few years later, in January 1996.

Bertrand's position was further validated when, in May 1996, federal Department of Justice officials intervened on Bertrand's behalf. Quebec's separatist government asked for a motion to dismiss the matter, arguing that secession was allowed if obtained by democratic consent. It also cited international law cases where secession was permitted for colonies or in cases where persons in a certain region of a country were persecuted. This was hardly the case in Canada. Even so, some separatists decried the federal intervention with Bertrand and actually claimed Canada was a prison and Quebec an oppressed colony.

York University constitutional lawyer Peter Hogg has said of unilateral declarations of independence, such as occurred in 1776 in the United States, that "the issue for the courts is simply whether or not the revolution has been successful." The issue, therefore, becomes whether the separatist government could convince the world, and the rest of Canada, that it was fully sovereign over its lands, politically and militarily.

In May 1996 Bouchard also argued that court cases did not matter, and that the will of the people would have to be acknowledged if in the next referendum a majority of Quebecers voted to leave Canada.

This type of argument is very dangerous for a democracy, because it allows constitutional rights to be scrapped by mere consent. It allowed the charismatic leader Benito Mussolini to convince Italians in the 1930s by plebiscite to scrap their constitution and democracy, thus paving the way for dictatorship and abrogation of constitutional rights.

As Harvard law professor Karl J. Friedrich warned, in his book *Constitutional Government and Democracy*: "The dictators of this century, following the example of Napoleon, have in turn relied on such referenda or plebiscites for legitimizing their unconstitutional and anti-constitutional regimes. Such direct popular approval provides an impressive facade for the dictatorial coup d'etat and can be used against democratic opposition at home and abroad on the pretext that 'the will of the people' has been consulted."

Another American journalist, Princeton University professor Herbert Agar, wrote about the same issue in his book, *The Perils of Democracy*: "If the will of the majority is held to be sovereign and supreme, overriding the written or unwritten constitution, why should the majority ever accept dismissal? It can easily rig a plebiscite, a meaningless Yes or No vote, which confirms its illicit power in the name of 'democracy'. The usurper becomes legitimate. The despotism springs from the 'people' who are henceforth silenced in the name of their own sovereign will. Walter Lippmann [American political commentator] calls this confusion between constitutional democracy and the mere will of the people 'the supreme political heresy of our time'. Yet it is an easy trick to play with language, as Hitler showed us, as plenty of 'bumpkins at the fair' fall for the trick every time."

Despite such arguments and historic precedents, both the separatists and the Quebec branch of the Liberal Party had party resolutions that stated that Quebec could secede from Canada any time it wanted.

A month after my Bouchard interview in November 1991, I attacked the separatists' dangerous strategy in a column in the *Post*. A majority-rules referendum triggering a unilateral declaration of independence would be unconstitutional. Canada could not allow Quebec's anglophones, allophones, and aboriginals to lose their citizenship rights if they did not want to lose them. According to the 1991 census, some 716,155 Quebecers use English at home and 362,695 use neither official language. Holding these Quebecers hostage would be "inviting violence," I speculated. Quebec separatists would be subjected to damaging trade sanctions by the rest of Canada, a stoppage of transfer payments and other government services. If the separatists went ahead and tried to leave, "Parizeau and his band of highwaymen would be deposed and arrested" because of their treasonous behaviour.

That column caused a firestorm in Quebec, unlike anything I'd written before or since. I was pilloried in cartoons in French and English. The Montreal *Gazette*'s cartoonist, Aislin, drew a perfume bottle shaped like a maple leaf with a bomb exploding on one side. The caption read: "And for that special Québécoise on your Christmas list 'Eau de

DIANE Francis' guaranteed to raise heated passion with that distinct Rosedalian 'je-ne-sais-pas-what-Quebec-really-wants' fragrance."

That month, *Chatelaine* magazine issued a press release naming me their 1992 "Woman of the Year." Almost immediately, *Chatelaine*'s Montreal offices (shared with *L'Actualité*) were deluged with complaints and had to be evacuated several times as a result of bomb threats by separatists. As part of its damage control, the French-language version of *Chatelaine* issued its own press release, which underscored the fact that it had selected a Quebecer as its "Woman of the Year."

Le Soleil then caricatured me as "La Canadienne de l'Année," scantily clad in a sado-masochistic outfit and whipping some poor man labelled "Quebec." Parizeau joked before thousands at a PQ conference that he was glad to be there and not in jail, because "Diane Francis was not prime minister."

The furore was due to the fact that the taboo against mentioning treason and violence had been broken by a ranking member of the Canadian establishment. It was one thing for a columnist to say incendiary things. It was quite another for the editor of one of the country's most influential national publications to say them. Attacks escalated and became personal. To separatist media, anyone who attacks Quebec or its politicians is an anti-French bigot or redneck. Anyone who mentions that separatist policies might cause violence or be illegal is inciting violence. Anyone who mentions kamikaze economics of separatism is called an "economic terrorist."

Fortunately, the separatists had no way to financially hurt the *Post*, *Maclean's*, or the English-language version of *Chatelaine*. After the bomb scares, Maclean Hunter's Quebec lieutenant and board member, Jean Paré, criticized me to executives and fellow directors. But it was to no avail. Then, months later, he suddenly quit writing a biweekly column for me in the *Post*. He had also been very upset with a column that I had written criticizing the separatists' "Je me souviens" or "I remember" guilt-trip message on Quebec's car licence plates, which had been changed from "La Belle Province." I questioned why English Canadians should be made to feel guilty about any past injustices by being reminded that Quebecers would "remember."

Another high-level lobbying effort was mounted in Britain at the *Financial Times* of London by influential persons unknown. I was labelled an "economic terrorist" and it was urged that I be removed. The *Financial Times* owned 19.9 percent of the *Post*. I never knew who my accuser or accusers were, but they came from the upper echelon of British, or European, society. And they failed.

Weeks later, after that controversy had died down, a Montreal *Gazette* reporter named Andrew McIntosh called, asking me to participate in a panel discussion on a Sunday in April 1992 at a journalists' symposium in Montreal. I declined at first, suspecting trouble. Then he got very aggressive with my assistant, Barb Maxwell, insisting that I couldn't write about arresting Parizeau without defending my statements in person.

The symposium was sponsored by the Fédération Professionnelle des Journalistes du Québec and was concerned with media coverage of constitutional matters. Mulroney had started a new round of constitutional talks, which culminated months later, in the fall of 1992, in the failed Charlottetown Accord referendum. The symposium pamphlet read: "Covering the Constitution: Are the media losing their grip?"

The guest list was impressive, drawn from the journalistic elite across the country. Bouchard and his Charlottetown Accord saleswoman, Tory Dorothy Dobbie, were among the blue-ribbon participants.

My panel session was on a Sunday afternoon and McIntosh picked me up at the airport. I assumed, incorrectly, that as an anglophone writer he would be sympathetic with my tough-mindedness towards separatists.

The event was staged in a theatre with steeply banked seats. Five of us sat on a dais, surrounded by a semi-circular assemblage of roughly two hundred or so interested onlookers. In front of each panellist was a microphone, for the lengthy question-and-answer period that was to follow our brief five-minute remarks off the top. It was tense and strangers stared. One pushed past without apology.

In the audience were "friendly" colleagues from English Canada's press, my former *Toronto Star* boss, John Honderich, and the *Star*'s Quebec City bureau chief, Bob Mackenzie. There were also my newspaper's Montreal correspondent, Kevin Doherty, and various other colleagues from the Ryerson journalism school, the CBC, the *Globe and Mail*, various western Canadian papers, and so on. The topic was: "Editorial writers and columnists: Is everything fair game?"

The proceedings kicked off when the moderator, a hot-headed separatist open-line radio show host, launched into a tirade about me. So did two francophone panellists in their five-minute speeches on the issue. The third panellist, a westerner, stuck to the topic. And I attacked the workshop itself.

"It's embarrassing that a group of journalists would even ask whether everything was fair game or not. We should be addressing how to extend freedom of speech, expression, press privileges," I told the audience.

The immoderate moderator opened the topic up to the audience for questions and for the next two hours not one question was directed at any of the other panellists. Quebec journalists queued up one after another to attack me and my columns, calling me names, shouting, insulting, ridiculing, and threatening action under the Hate Propaganda section of the Criminal Code. One questioner suggested I return to the United States and start another civil war there. Another said that as an immigrant I had no knowledge of Canadian history and of what English Canada owed French Canada. Others criticized the fact that the *Financial Post* would appoint an editor who could not read, write, or speak French.

The other panellists said nothing. English-Canadian journalists in the audience said nothing. To add insult to injury, the *Star*'s Mackenzie feverishly took notes and wrote an unfair, unflattering news story about me and my flogging the next day. So did a number of other publications.

To my accusers, I kept repeating what I believe the law states: that the constitution prohibits unilateral declarations of independence, because this would breach the protection of those Canadians within Quebec who do not want to leave. They had a right to protection and to their citizenship. There are rules to protect citizens from political populism or whims. This, I told them, was the basis of civilized nations. A referendum should never overrule a constitution. This was what Benito Mussolini had done in Italy: he convinced Italians in a plebiscite to democratically overthrow their own democracy.

But the crowd wanted blood and got some. Later I learned that while I was being pummelled verbally, McGill University law professor Stephen Scott was outside the session, trying to get organizers to let him hand out information that supported my stance, that the separatists couldn't just leave Canada without the permission of all Canadians through a constitutional amendment.

Scott had been pilloried by these same Quebec separatists in the media about a year earlier after making similar remarks. He predicted there would be violence if separatists wrested the province away without the permission of all its residents. He had been asked to participate in a Fraser Institute symposium on North American federalism after Meech Lake had died. It caused a similar controversy because his comments were reported in the prestigious *New York Times*: "Professor Scott surprised the Montreal conference when he suggested that 'the use of the limited amount of force needed to retain the sparsely inhabited territories of Northern Quebec would probably be effective to frustrate any attempt by Quebec to secede.' It was one of the rare times in the constitutional debate that any allusion to military force or coercion has been heard."

La Presse called Scott's remarks part of a "federal conspiracy" to frighten Quebecers away from their rightful nationalism. And a cadre of columnists flailed away at Scott for weeks afterward, just as they had flailed away at me for weeks.

"That was the first time I spoke publicly on these issues in many years and when an anglophone steps out of line like this, a tantrum is always thrown," Scott explained to me later. "The tantrum has two purposes: one, to reassure the public that the ideas are so outrageous that they can't be taken seriously, and two, to send a message to the Rest of Canada that the ideas if put forward will infuriate Quebecers. The next technique is to ignore, censor, and freeze out critics."

And that's exactly what the symposium did: it beat me up verbally and censored Scott.

"The clerks at the registration desk of the symposium referred me to the person who, they said, was in charge (a francophone man, thirtyish, whose name I do not know)," recalled Scott. "I was refused permission to give out the documents even though this conference was about accuracy and fairness in coverage about the constitution."

The ordeal ended and I took an early flight home to Toronto. In the Rapidair waiting area, a CBC producer whose name I've forgotten came over. His sentiments were very touching. "I just wanted to extend my condolences. You did a terrific job back there. I don't know how you could stand all that abuse. I just wanted to say that."

The separatist bullies pulled it off. The next day, I wrote about how vicious the symposium had been. But I did not write another controversial column about Quebec separatism for two more years. Then, in the spring of 1994, Stephen Scott brought some friends from Montreal to see me.

3
Resurrection

In April 1994 Stephen Scott and members of the Equality Party said they were coming to Toronto and wanted to meet with my editorial board at the *Post*. The Equality Party was an anglophone rights group and held one seat in Quebec's National Legislative Assembly. A time was set and the meeting was attended by four Equality Party spokesmen, my two editorial board members as well as the Toronto *Sun's* two editorial writers.

The Montrealers had just held a press conference in Toronto where they had trotted out a press release signed by prominent experts such as historian Michael Bliss and former Saskatchewan premier Allan Blakeney, who had become a law professor. These notables had signed a document saying that the constitution forbade unilateral declarations of independence.

The publicity stunt produced little ink in the press, but they were still happy to have their opinions validated outside the province by experts. Meanwhile, their purpose at the *Post* editorial board was to convince journalists outside

Quebec to take up the cause. They were worried that the Parti Québécois would win the next provincial election and put into motion their plans to unilaterally secede. They were concerned that this would result in violence, and that the rest of Canada was not aware of such a danger. They were also concerned, as were most of us, with Bouchard's recent trips to New York City to meet with United Nations secretary-general Boutros Boutros-Ghali and to Washington D.C. to meet with U.S. officials. They felt these trips were damaging because they gave the impression that separation would somehow be blessed internationally.

I chaired the editorial board but spent five minutes describing to my peers what had happened to me two years before at the Montreal symposium. I was still upset.

Then Stephen Scott took the floor and handed out a pamphlet about constitutional law he had written. One of Canada's most prominent constitutional experts, Scott had been tenacious in taking on the separatists and the Quebec media.

"I have been bashed about, but I'm reasonably independent," he explained. A Montrealer who has been at McGill for years, he is fluently bilingual and has never considered leaving. "I guess I've been hurt in that I don't get a lot of government consultations. I don't get many invites because I'm not politically correct."

The meeting was interesting, but the other journalists were sceptical. After all, it appeared to be just another confusing case of one legal interpretation versus another. The separatists had also trotted out their "experts" on constitutional law, who claimed that a referendum could justify separation because it would represent the democratic wishes of an electorate. But Scott insisted that was wrong. He explained to us why the issue of the constitution, which bored Canadians from coast to coast, was so important.

"The importance of establishing the legalities here has been because no one in Ottawa has ever called the separatists' bluff or even contradicted statements by them. The separatists say if a majority of Quebecers opt to leave they can simply leave," said Scott. "That is just not true, under the law, which means that Quebec No voters would be entitled to defy the new government and be justified in asking for the army to step in to protect their citizenship. The problem has been that the separatists have not been contradicted, and they have been allowed to make Quebecers think that there would be no problem if they voted to leave."

The illegality of unilateral secession was eventually established by Guy Bertrand in 1995. Of course, it represented a gigantic leap from an illegal act by a province to sending in troops to quell a revolutionary regime in Quebec City.

Scott's opinion, untested at the time, appeared extreme. After all, if this was true why hadn't the federal government stated this? After all, for three decades three Quebec prime ministers, Pierre Trudeau, Brian Mulroney, and Jean Chrétien, told English Canada there was a Quebec problem, a constitutional problem, and they could fix it. So English Canadians voted for Quebec national leaders. But the problem just got worse, never better.

And while these prime ministers were busy appeasing separatists and selling English Canada on that concept, they were all turning a blind eye to the linguistic discrimination imposed by Quebec on its sizeable anglophone minority, as Scott pointed out. Not once did any of these prime ministers exercise their constitutional right to disallow discriminatory Quebec laws—not even in 1986 after the Supreme Court of Canada found that banning English on outdoor signs violated the Charter of Rights and Freedoms. Then-Premier Robert Bourassa invoked the "nothwithstanding" clause, which allowed him to ignore the court's ruling for five years. But few Canadians realized that Prime Minister Mulroney could have overruled Bourassa's "notwithstanding" manoeuvre by simply invoking the federal power to disallow. He may not have because he wanted Bourassa to support his Meech Lake initiative, or because it would have brought about a great opportunity for separatists to whip up anti-Canada sentiment in Quebec. Or he may not have because of opinions such as those expressed by York University's Peter Hogg, who said: "In my view . . . the modern development of ideas of judicial review and democratic responsibility has left no room for the exercise of the federal power of disallowance."

Trudeau was another matter. He should have disallowed the first seriously discriminatory law passed in 1974. But he chose not to because it was politically embarrassing: the provincial branch of the Liberals had authored that law, out of fear that if they did not the separatists would win the next election.

The separatists won anyway in 1976 and went even further. But Trudeau still didn't have the guts to disallow it, because he wanted the separatists to lose the upcoming 1980 referendum on sovereignty-association. He admitted this strategy in a letter sent on February 27, 1979 to an anglophone rights group called the Freedom of Choice Movement.

"My colleagues and I are also very concerned about the oppressive and divisive measures in this legislation. We concluded that disallowance or immediate referral to the Supreme Court would be a serious error. This kind of active intervention would offer the Parti Québécois an opportunity to distract attention from the bill itself to the question of whether they, as the elected government, have the right to legislate in matters of provincial responsibility. This would certainly be exploited in the referendum campaign. We have spoken out against Bill 101 and will continue to do so. We believe that the majority of Quebecers do not share the aims of the Parti Québécois."

In essence, Trudeau was trying to finesse the separatists by acceding to their oppressive law in order to win the upcoming 1980 referendum on sovereignty-association. So he and his Liberals sacrificed the anglo minority in Quebec and the separatists were given free rein to impose even more unfair measures in ensuing years.

The damage had been incalculable. People's lives had been disrupted. Families split. The economy of the country's most important city, Montreal, had been reduced to back-water status.

Trudeau's failure to fight Bill 101 sparked a mass migration out of Quebec. Gigantic Sun Life Assurance left and the rest of the country's financial establishment followed. An estimated 120,000 anglos and hundreds of head offices migrated else-where between 1976 and 1986, according to press reports and census figures on population flows. Over the past thirty years a total of 300,000 anglos have left the province. Despite the unfairness, English Canadians as a whole did not get up in arms over the issue. That is because these people were not looked upon as political refugees (though that is what they were) because they were not really the kind of victims that arouse sympathy. After all, they were Quebec's most well-heeled and mobile citizens. Besides, some of us thought that perhaps these people were not tolerant towards French and were better off living elsewhere.

"In the absence of anyone enforcing the constitution of this country, the separatists have simply kept pushing to see how far they can go, and they will keep pushing until they separate," said Equality Party leader Keith Henderson to the joint editorial board.

The journalists were also unwilling to think about vio-lence. After all, Canada was not the United States, which had fought a bloody civil war for four years with southern separatists. Equality's Henderson explained how the vio-lence would surface.

"There will be violence if the separatists go ahead and declare the province is a separate country. The violence hap-pens in this way: the separatists win a Yes in a referendum and tell everyone in Quebec to start sending their sales and income taxes to Quebec City instead of Ottawa. Supposing nearly half of Quebecers vote No and do not accept that they have lost their birthright. So they continue to send their taxes to Ottawa. Not everybody can move to Toronto or Vancouver or the States. Does Quebec sue these people in the courts? What do the judges do? Whom do they owe their allegiance to, and if a judge also realizes that separation is illegal is the judge arrested? And by whom? Does Quebec become a police state and, if so, what does Canada do? Does the province send in police to collect taxes from Canadian citizens? And when does Ottawa move into Quebec to protect those citizens from Quebec police? Do you see what we mean?"

Few in that room were convinced that this was anything more than a very hypothetical, if logical, line of argument. Few were convinced that these guys were anything more than cranks who were exaggerating the so-called abuses against anglophones in Quebec. And if things were so bad, why were so many anglos still living there happily? Weren't most of the 300,000 anglos who left in the 1970s just bigots, as the separatists claimed? Those who left could because they were wealthy or occupationally mobile. There would be no tag days for the Montreal diaspora.

As for violence, everyone in the room felt that at the end of the day a political deal would be cut and Stephen Scott and other constitutional wonks could argue all they liked. Even if the courts ruled separation unconstitutional and the separatists defied the court order, no Quebec-born prime minister would order in the troops. It was unimaginable. So a deal would be struck.

One journalist who attended later described the Equality Party as "language loonies." The Equality Party began formally in 1989 and overtook a predecessor group, called the Freedom of Choice Movement, a protest group that formed to fight the first anti-English language laws.

After a highly successful first election in 1989, when the party won four seats in the provincial legislature, the Equality Party had one setback after another. Its reputation was badly hurt when its leader, Robert Libman, left the fold to try to get into the rival Liberal Party. Another did the same, and the last straw was when an Equality MNA actually joined the hated Parti Québécois. That left only Neil Cameron in 1994 as a sitting Equality member.

These embarrassments were discussed at the meeting.

But Cameron and Henderson said they were not interested in publicity for their party. They simply wanted English Canadians to realize that Parizeau was likely to be elected in a few months and to stage another referendum that could win. Following that the separatists would call Canada's bluff and unilaterally declare independence.

At that meeting was another key Equality Party member, Andrew Male. Like most Equality Party members he was a masochist, a believer in lost causes. But Male worked tirelessly for the cause, because he said he had been blacklisted by separatists. He had been fired as editor of Bombardier Inc.'s in-house publication in 1992 for political reasons and had lived off his wrongful-termination settlement since.

"When I was fired I wasn't even involved politically. I was a lapsed Equality Party member, but I knew Neil Cameron," said Andrew. "Neil sent a letter to her [the supervisor who fired Andrew] congratulating me on the content of my magazine and my boss just went nuts, freaking out. I guessed she was a separatist and hated the Equality Party. All I know is that a few days later I was fired even though I was on sick leave for depression because my mother was dying of cancer."

Andrew is prematurely grey and looks older than his thirty-seven years. He is inhumanly tenacious, issuing press releases and cultivating sympathetic media coverage. Once a journalist is in his Rolodex, he or she can expect calls night or day with the latest developments or new information. Even over a few beers, talk always turns to politics.

"I would love to have a normal life, but I've been blacklisted," he said. "I cannot get a job in the aerospace industry because of the francization policies of companies and what happened at Bombardier. I cannot get a job in the public sector in my province because anglophones are rarely hired by the provincial government."

Male was correct about anglos being unable to find jobs in the public sector. Requirements to work strictly in French in the provincial government have allowed wholesale discrimination in hiring practices. As of 1990, less than 1 percent of the entire Quebec civil service was of English-speaking origin, and only 1.8 percent of the most senior ranks, wrote University of Toronto historian Robert Bothwell in an article titled "Out Damn Spot," part of a book containing a collection of pieces about Quebec. By contrast some 15 percent of Quebec residents speak English at home, according to the 1991 Census of Canada.

For me, the meeting with Equality was to be a turning point. Their message got through. But not to the others, who never wrote about anything that was discussed. They were understandably reluctant to break the taboos about violence and treason.

While some of the Equality arguments seemed exaggerated, they were reminiscent of an interview I had in the mid-1980s with an ex-Quebecer, Oscar Rajsky, owner of shirt manufacturer John Forsyth Limited. He had fled Europe after surviving the Holocaust and immigrated to Montreal, where he became successful after the war in Montreal's garment industry. At the time of the interview in 1982, he employed several thousand persons and mentioned how he had moved the entire company to Toronto from Montreal after the separatists' election in 1976. "I left because I won't tolerate another bunch of Nazis. The guys in that Parti [Québécois] are anti-Semitic, anti-English, and socialists. To me, they are the French-Canadian version of the Nazis," he said.

At the time, I thought he was exaggerating. So would have most of Canada's media.

"What happened here in Quebec to our linguistic and other rights has been ignored by the national media," said Stephen Scott. "These ideas are not politically correct. The French nationalists are politically correct. Listen to Peter Gzowski's panels on Quebec and no matter what Quebec nationalists do to people it's glossed over because in his type of cracker-barrel journalism everyone is well-intentioned and the tough points are neither made nor asked.

"Fundamentally, you excepted of course, Canadian journalism is a journalism that doesn't want to ask the tough questions or make the hard points. It's full of lefties, trendies, the touchy-feelies and the warm and fuzzies. People like us are dangerous to them. And people like us are treated like social pariahs too," added Scott.

My next column dealt with the fact that the separatists had no intention of paying their fair share of the national debt if they ever left. Parizeau had made that quite clear to me in interviews. The point of repeating his threats was to emphasize that this would never be tolerated by English Canadians. Parizeau said there was nothing that English Canada could do about it, but I published a solution. I suggested that if an attempt was made by Parizeau to avoid obligations, the Bank of Canada should simply issue a press release to bondholders stating that it would pay principal and interest on 75.5 percent of the bonds but that Quebec would be on the hook for the rest.

The separatists disdained such ideas, as did one Bay Street big shot who said such action would be considered a default by Canada. But that would not be the case if the Bank of Canada made it very clear that from a certain date onward, if Quebec left, the debt would be split proportionately. He argued that it would make Canadian bonds unsaleable with the prospect of that hanging over their issuance, but my point was that unless Canada talked tough the separatists could tell Quebecers that there would be no objection from English Canada about debt repayments.

Another point I made in that column was that the separatists could not go it alone unless they got out from under their portion of debts. At 1994 debt figures, Quebec's provincial plus federal debt was 122 percent of its entire economic output. Its interest payments were equivalent to 353.6 percent of its exports, compared to Alberta's 106.9 percent or Ontario's 184.6 percent. Furthermore, I added that Quebec could be forced to pay its share because it needed English Canada more than vice versa. Some 26.5 percent of its manufacturing shipments went to the rest of

Canada by the late 1980s compared with only 6.8 percent the other way around. Canada should make threats: a trade boycott or veto over NAFTA membership, so if the separatists were unreasonable they could be economically isolated. These points were repeated.

To drive these arguments home and generate understanding and debate among members of the public and political elite, a credible French-Canadian spokesperson was needed and when I asked Paul Desmarais Sr. for an interview, he agreed. He was the richest French Canadian in the world. I flew to Montreal in May 1994 and arrived in Power Corporation's elegant, mansion-like offices. The man at the security desk buzzed Desmarais's secretary. Minutes later, she appeared out of the elevators with a worried look on her face. She had been frantically trying to reach me while I was in transit.

"Mr. Desmarais does not want you to meet him in his offices. He does not want people to know that you are talking to him. He is at home and he will talk to you there. Here is a cab slip with the address and I will help you get a cab," she said.

Desmarais is a great Canadian success story. A poor francophone from Ontario, he bought a bankrupt bus company and parlayed that into an empire worth billions. Not only was Desmarais powerful financially, but he was Canada's most politically-plugged-in tycoon. One of his sons married Prime Minister Jean Chretién's daughter. His right-hand man was John Rae, Ontario Premier Bob Rae's brother. He had Brian Mulroney and Liberal Senator Michael Pitfield on his payroll. He also controlled a media empire in Quebec, including the largest French language daily, *La Presse*.

His Westmount home was exquisite but deceptive. From the street, the stone house looked sprawling enough, but its true size was hidden. It tumbled several stories down the hillside with a spectacular view of downtown Montreal.

The houseboy welcomed me into a foyer filled with exquisite sculptures and paintings. Desmarais sat sipping coffee in a cheerful sunroom decorated in bright kelly green and lemon yellow. Behind him were latticed floor-to-ceiling windows overlooking the city skyline and terraced gardens and swimming pool two floors below.

Before we began a two-hour discussion, Desmarais said he had decided against an on-the-record interview. Things were very difficult in Quebec and going to get worse. He and his family could be harmed and intimidated if he was outspoken. This happened during the October Crisis in 1970. He had to hire bodyguards for himself and his family and relocate for a lengthy period of time to Florida until things cooled off. But he was passionately concerned about what was happening and several times he said out loud to no one in particular: "Who is going to fight for Canada?"

It was frustrating. A compromise was reached. He'd talk and have a veto over whatever was written before publication. It was worth a shot to get a hard-hitting column based on tough talk from someone as important and influential as Desmarais. That would encourage others in Quebec to stand up to the separatists, including his relative by marriage, the prime minister.

He was faxed the column for his comments and suggestions. He personally called back and asked that the column be killed. It was. That was unfortunate, but the interview reinforced my view that the separatists were not the champions of all French Canadians. Here was Paul Desmarais Sr., the most successful self-made French Canadian in the world, and he despised the separatists. And vice versa. Yet even the powerful Desmarais was intimidated by his own elected leaders. Everybody was being held hostage by the separatists.

Desmarais inspired my next editorial salvo: "Parti Québécois leader Jacques Parizeau does not represent a grassroots movement by francophones for self-determination. Such a claim is a sham and Parizeau's latest actions prove it." Parizeau was the political equivalent of a corporate predator who had failed for thirty years to make an unfriendly takeover, I wrote. Parizeau's problem was that the "shareholders" were not willing to give up their assets.

Around this time Parizeau announced that he would consider a victory in the upcoming fall provincial election as a mandate to secede. He said he would declare the intention to leave and negotiate a deal, if possible. Then he said a separate referendum months later would be held to merely bless the new constitution and terms of exit. Weeks later, he did a complete about-face after polls told him that he would lose his lead if he turned the election into a referendum for separation. He said a referendum would be held a few months after the election.

Meanwhile Bouchard was running around as a self-appointed external affairs minister for Quebec. He was visiting capitals and politicians in other countries, selling separatism to the world. For instance, he had met with UN secretary-general Boutros Boutros-Ghali weeks before, giving the impression the UN official somehow endorsed Quebec separatism. Boutros Boutros-Ghali had posed for a photograph with Bouchard but I thought he looked distinctly uncomfortable at the time. My perception turned out to be correct.

The UN offices in New York City were dingy and unimpressive. Corridors needed a paint job and the offices were cheaply furnished, as befits a cash-starved organization. An academic from Egypt with impeccable British manners and flawless English, Boutros-Ghali was clearly cognizant of the delicacy of the matters to be discussed in this interview. At his request, some general questions were faxed to him before the interview. He certainly did not want to wade into the internal affairs of a ranking, and dues-paying, member of the UN. But I did.

On the other hand, it was obvious that he felt somewhat manipulated by Bouchard and wanted to set the record straight. And he also wanted an opportunity to talk about UN peacekeeping efforts and to appeal for financial help. The UN, at that point, was virtually bankrupt and under siege from members who felt its bureaucracy was bloated and ineffectual.

The secretary general confirmed that his agreement to meet with Bouchard did not mean he blessed the cause. "It does not mean any kind of acceptance," he said candidly. "Any official who wants to see me I have to see. Supposing I did not want to see him. That would mean I was intervening in the internal affairs of a member state. Unless the member state asks me to intervene, I cannot intervene."

And while he would not comment specifically on Canadian internal affairs, he did question what he dubbed "micro-nationalism" or the division along ethnic lines of countries into small entities. This struck at the heart of the separatists' self-determation argument—a concept that separatists like to trot out as justification for breaking away. "Self-determination" is a concept endorsed in principle by the UN, but Boutros Boutros-Ghali argued that this applied to colonies, not to provinces. Of course, the separatist cant has always been that Quebec is a colony and needs liberation.

Interestingly, Boutros-Ghali specialized as an academic in the issue of minority self-determination. "[Minority] self-determination is one of the most tricky subjects. It is very complicated, difficult, and significant. If each minority asks for self-determination, rather than 184 nations around the world, we may have five hundred to one thousand countries in the world, and that is not in the interests of peace or economic development.

"Furthermore, what do people mean by minority self-determination? You still find another minority within the minority. You never solve the minority rights issue by this means [independence]," he said.

He said that is why "micronationalism" is flawed. In Yugoslavia, there are minorities within minorities and the entire country has now been partitioned into dozens of ethnically homogeneous pieces. Even after the fighting stops, the region will be ungovernable and economically unviable, he said.

He drew a comparison between Yugoslavia and Quebec. For anti-separatist purposes, Canada as Bosnia North was a frightening and instructive spectre. Quebec, like Yugoslavia, was not homogeneous. There were the anglos in Montreal and the aboriginals in the upper two-thirds of the province.

To further investigate the point about partition, I knew I had to interview Cree Chief Matthew Coon-Come. We spoke on the telephone, and the chief spent ninety minutes articulating his stand on the matter. He told me where he would draw his line in the sand.

Coon-Come suggested that the Cree would boycott any referendum on Quebec separation (which they did in October 1995, by holding their own), ignore a Yes outcome and ask for protection from the Canadian Armed Forces if secession were attempted.

"I would call upon the people of Canada to be the watchdog. I would call upon the international community to act as a watchdog to ensure that there's no gross violation of basic fundamental human rights. It would be up to Canada to determine how to exercise its constitutional responsibility should Quebec try to go," said the chief.

"I'll do all the things I can to avoid any violence. My people are not violent people and never raised arms in opposition to the Great Whale [hydroelectric] project. We have always taken the legal avenue or [worked] through public relations, debates and forums. That's been our strategy."

He said he was going to take his case to European and American politicians, to set the record straight following similar visits by Bouchard. He said he wanted foreigners to know that the 12,000 Cree living from the forty-ninth to the fifty-fifth parallels will never accept separation as proposed by Bouchard and Parizeau.

This was the first time that violence was threatened by any of Quebec's minorities. Coon-Come also agreed with the Equality Party that if Quebec could leave Canada, parts of Quebec could leave Quebec. The Inuit, who occupied the northern one-third of the province, agreed and were also likely to boycott the referendum. As things turned out, both aboriginal groups staged their own referendums days before the October 30, 1995, vote, and roughly 96 percent of each first nation voted No.

"They [separatists] talk about the right to self-determination," Coon-Come told me. "I want to clarify that only if people's human rights are gravely violated, and there is no recourse in courts, would they have the legal right under international law to secede from a recognized state.

"There are no serious violations by the Canadian government of human rights in Quebec. For decades, the prime ministers have been from Quebec. French Canadians are represented in cabinet, in Parliament, in the judiciary. Quebec gets billions a year from Ottawa. Wanting to get Manpower and Immigration from the federal government to the provincial government has nothing to do with violations of basic human rights," he added.

"There is also a question here of a double standard. We raise this because Quebec thinks it has different rules for native peoples and different rules for Quebecers. Look at Parizeau when he tries to justify the current borders of Quebec. He says native people surrendered their rights in 1975 [in the land-claims settlement concerning James Bay]. But Quebec surrendered rights when it joined Confederation in 1867.

"Parizeau classifies the Crees as [just another] minority. There is a difference. Aboriginal rights are in the Constitution. There are treaties. The government has no treaties with the Greeks or the Jews," he said.

He also, quite rightly, criticized the Liberals for mishandling separatism. "As long as the government of Canada is silent on their position and their strategy, should Quebec secede from Canada, and as long as Bloc Québécois leader Lucien Bouchard is allowed to make statements that are not true, and nobody's contesting it, we will have only ourselves to blame for what might happen.

"The Liberal government [in Quebec] created the Bélanger-Campeau Commission that looked at possible secession. So they've entertained those scenarios, opening up a discussion they would like to deny now.

"We must have this debate now so we won't let the separatists set the agenda or make these ridiculous statements. If all this is discussed at the eleventh hour, it's going to be too late. There is too much at stake. I feel the Cree nation as a people have the fundamental right of self-determination. It's not a question of the Cree seceding from Quebec but Quebec seceding from Canada and the Crees. If the entire landscape is to be changed, then the Cree people should have the right to determine their own status."

The chief's main argument was that the government must protect its citizens, but it has not done so. His people were saying what Ottawa should have been saying: that an independent Quebec without permission from all governments in the country was an illegal, or revolutionary, government, and the Cree would request armed protection. They also wanted the right to determine their own future status. They were, in essence, asking for a Bosnian-style partitioning.

The column based on my interview with the Cree chief ended with a quote along these lines from Desmarais, although I didn't name him: "Civilization is a varnish. Scratch away the varnish and you have human nature. You have Bosnia, Northern Ireland, Oka, Chiapas, and on and on. To think that Canadians have never been violent when they perceive their rights and interests are involved is very, very naive."

The rest of the media in Canada ignored this bombshell interview. But Parizeau certainly did not. Just three months later he became premier and retained the Indian and Northern Affairs portfolio for himself in a bid to co-opt the aboriginals. It wouldn't work.

The country was headed for a serious showdown. Parizeau won in the fall of 1994, and as 1995 began, the newly crowned Premier Parizeau and Bouchard were talking hard-line separatism and plotting their referendum. Then, on September 7, 1995, the campaign began—a campaign that very nearly ended the country.

4
The Lobsters

It was an open secret during the summer of 1995 that the referendum would be held soon. But before the legislation was tabled, with its confusing referendum question, Parizeau nearly blew his cause. He made an arrogant off-the-record remark at a closed-door session with the European Union's fifteen ambassadors posted to Canada. The diplomats wanted to be briefed by Parizeau about the upcoming referendum and various scenarios. Never one to pass up an elegant meal or an opportunity to pontificate, Parizeau was thoroughly candid and told the Europeans that a Yes vote was going to be an irrevocable vote for the separation of Quebec. It was not going to be a renewed partnership or some halfway measures. He flippantly said that Quebec Yes voters would be like lobsters in a lobster trap: once inside, they would not be able to get out no matter how hard they tried. It was a telling remark.

"Now we have the policy of the lobster pot," wrote *Gazette* anglophone rights champion William Johnson. "Whether the water is cold and salty or soft and boiling, once past the trap door there is no going back, or so Premier Parizeau now says. The association with Canada, presented as a condition of sovereignty-association in 1980, is now reduced to the status of bait to entice the unwary into the trap."

But his criticism was the usual one-day wonder. Stories wash over the Québécois press all the time, because the separatist intelligentsia close ranks and immediately go about the business of damage control. This usually involves a spate of contrary op-ed pieces by separatist academics or spin doctors, a campaign of letters to the editor or string of columnists or commentators who confuse, tone down, or attack criticism. By escalating the news noise, the separatists dilute the negative impact.

Over the years, these propaganda techniques resulted in a soft-soaping of the separatist ideology, which attracted Quebecers who simply wanted a better deal within Canada. These moderates were Parizeau's lobsters.

And the trap was being set. Just six weeks before the referendum, *Gazette* columnist and former politician Nick Auf Der Maur gave the public their first glimpse of the separatist dirty tricks about to be played.

"The Péquistes are starting in August an enumerators' training course. Some Péquiste strategists believe they might be able to gain two or three percentage points in the referendum just by making it difficult for ethnics and anglos to get on the list. They will operate on the assumption that people with funny-sounding names are not Canadian citizens, and thus ineligible to vote. The PQ won't admit it but one of its objectives in setting up these training courses for enumerators is to keep as many anglos and ethnics off the electoral list [as possible]."

Even on the heels of such revelations, the separatists boldly tabled Bill One—An Act Respecting the Future of Quebec. It contained the wording of the referendum question: "Do you agree that Quebec should become sovereign, after having made a formal offer to Canada for a new economic and political partnership, within the scope of the bill respecting the future of Quebec and of the agreement signed on June 12, 1995?"

The "agreement" signed in June was a three-way pact between Bouchard, Parizeau, and Mario Dumont, leader of an upstart party that had broken off from the youth wing of the Liberals. Who knew what the "agreement" was? It could have been interpreted as a Yes vote in favour of an agreement with Ottawa. The question was cunningly confusing.

"The question was a fraud. They lied to convince someone of something they wouldn't want to be. It was a trick question," said Quebec City lawyer and former separatist Guy Bertrand. He personally took the province to court to challenge Bill One's constitutionality and have the referendum stopped. He did not succeed. "It was designed to make some people think we'd stay in Canada."

A poll later showed that 16 percent of Yes voters thought the new partnership with Canada had already been signed and they were simply blessing it and 29 percent of Yes voters thought Quebec would stay a province.

Bertrand, a former high-ranking separatist, was opposed to separation. He had run for the PQ leadership and his brother, Rosaire Bertrand, was the head of the party's caucus in Quebec City. But Guy Bertrand left the separatist movement in the fall of 1994 when he said he realized that Quebec had enough protections, that it was mistreating its anglophone minority by ignoring constitutional rights, and that independence would be suicide and unnecessary.

Bertrand knew all the tricks. He had been constitutional adviser to René Lévesque, and knew that the Equality Party was right. The declaration of unilateral independence was illegal, but they were going to bluff it out. Because all three prime ministers were too frightened to take them on head to head, they were confident they could pull it off. Bertrand took matters into his own hands in 1995 because he knew the federalists would not mount a legal challenge.

The referendum legislation outlined the voting rules. Yes and No committees were appointed and any advertising had to be approved by them. If the Yes forces won, Quebec's government had one year to negotiate an acceptable arrangement with Ottawa. If this was not accomplished, then Quebec would declare independence.

Bertrand asked the federal government to intervene and help win the case. Justice Minister Allan Rock and Prime Minister Chrétien refused. Fortunately, Bertrand won a partial victory before the referendum ended. The court ruled that Quebec could not secede on the basis of a majority vote in a referendum by Quebecers. Any change in the status of its citizens had to be blessed by an amendment to the constitution. This meant that the House of Commons and the legislatures of at least seven provinces with 50 percent or more of the population had to agree to separation.

Bertrand convinced the court that the separatists jeopardized his fundamental rights under the Charter of Rights and Freedoms, particularly the right to move within Canada, to vote, and to hold a Canadian passport.

The judge agreed that the legislation was unconstitutional because it circumvented charter rights without a proper amendment to the constitution. In essence, the judge stated uncategorically that no Canadian could be stripped of his passport, vote, or right to move within the country without a constitutional amendment.

But the judge declined to impose an injunction that would have stopped the referendum. He explained this by saying that while any unilateral declaration of independence was unconstitutional, there was no law against the vote itself. It was, essentially, a poll taken on an "illegal" process.

At that point, the federal government should have done something to derail the process. It could have invoked its power to disallow Bill One, thus ending the referendum on the basis that it was linked to an unconstitutional act. It could have disallowed part of the legislation. It could have heavily criticized the process. It could have joined Bertrand in his constitutional challenge (which it eventually did, months later, in May 1996). It could have mounted its own court challenge on portions of the legislation. Instead, Ottawa did nothing.

A group of Equality Party officials and other federalists, who had formed the Special Committee for Canadian Unity, wanted to to tell Quebecers that the separatists had plotted an illegal act and did not care about individual rights.

But the No Committee, run by Liberals and Tories and prominent federalist businessmen, refused the Special Committee permission to advertise or to tap provincial government funds available to any approved advertiser. The Liberals wanted to control the political approach and quashed any attempts at hard-line tactics or an approach that they did not agree with totally. Rebuffed, the Special Committee complained to a referendum tribunal set up as a watchdog over the process, claiming that they had a legitimate right to participate in the No campaign by denouncing the illegality of the separatists' plans. The tribunal agreed with the Special Committee's complaint just three days before the referendum vote was taken. The No Committee offered it a paltry $2,500. But it was too little too late.

The No Committee also purposely ignored information brought to its attention that would have greatly embarrassed Bouchard and the Yes side. On September 30, I reproduced a copy of a personal letter sent to me from Canada's Secretary of State for Citizenship and Immigration in the 1980s when I became a Canadian citizen.

> ...Your Government is pleased that of all the nations of the world, you have chosen Canada as your new home. This is an important day for you and for Canada. From this point forward, as a Canadian citizen, you will share fully in the rights and privileges enjoyed by all Canadians. At the same time, you assume the special responsibility of protecting and preserving the principles of democracy and human freedom which are the cornerstones of our nation.
>
> [Signed] Sincerely,
> Lucien Bouchard

Reaction was dramatic and the column was faxed all across the country. One company printed five thousand copies and handed them out to customers, suppliers, and the public. I had found the letter the year before and saved it for the referendum to maximize its impact. No Committee members were urged to use it in their advertisements to discredit Bouchard. They never did.

I also publicly challenged Bouchard to resign if his side lost, which he had urged the prime minister to do during the referendum campaign. Bouchard's strategy was simple. He wanted the prime minister to commit to resign if the Yes side obtained 50 percent plus one, for two reasons. First, it would legitimize a simple-majority outcome as a mandate to separate even though it was unconstitutional. And second, a resignation would bring about a federal election, immobilize the government while that lasted, and result in a backlash among English-Canadian voters that would be helpful in convincing French Quebecers they were unwanted.

I suggested that the converse of the proposal should also be binding, and faxed Bouchard the following question, which I promised to publish: "Given your opinion that the prime minister must resign if there is a 50 percent plus one Yes outcome, you obviously intend to resign if there is a 50 percent plus one No outcome. True or false, Lucien?"

He never replied. And the prime minister never challenged Bouchard to resign after losing the referendum. He also failed to challenge the dirty enumeration tricks that were starting to surface during the campaign. Under Quebec's rigged rules, enumerators (one from the PQ and one Liberal) were to visit each home to register voters. Residents had to convince enumerators they were citizens by showing proof, but the catch was that either enumerator could strike anyone from the voters' list if he or she suspected the person was not a citizen. The onus was then on the disenfranchised voter, who was formally notified of being struck from the list, to go to a "revision" office with evidence of citizenship.

The rules were a sham. Why would PQ enumerators agree to put someone on a list then take him or her off at the eleventh hour? It made no sense, except to the separatists. They undoubtedly eliminated many potential No voters who were taken off the list, did not realize it had happened, or could not go to a "revision" office to get back on the list.

The injustice of this process was pointed out eloquently in a letter that I quoted in a *Maclean's* column during the campaign. "My mother, a hale and hearty 81, is residing in a seniors' residence, having voted in innumerable elections and more than one referendum," wrote her son, Lyman Canning, of Baie d' Urfe.

"She has no passport, as she has never travelled off the continent. She has no citizenship papers; none were ever needed. She is a native-born Canadian. She does not have a copy of her birth certificate. In the Quebec of 1914, birth and death records were kept, as in this case, at small rural Protestant churches, many of which are now closed, making records difficult to obtain. None were needed, until now. I do not think my mother's case is unique. Should we imagine possible dirty tricks, given that most seniors will tend to vote No?"

A nursing home operator, Juliette Ashburn of Notre Dame de Grace, told the *Gazette* a Quebec enumerator refused to register some of her elderly patients on the basis they were "incompetent" because they could not remember the year of their birth. Her complaints led officials to send enumerators back and all residents were registered. The problem, however, remains that their names could still be removed in the weeks leading up to the referendum. (And unless they checked the rolls they would have found they could not vote on referendum day.)

To correct this injustice, people had to realize what happened and then produce proof of citizenship. These rules clearly disenfranchised shut-ins, illiterates, and persons who didn't speak or read English or French, as well as sick and disabled persons. It also placed an unfair burden upon the working population. The legislation contained no requirement for employers to give workers time off or to pay them if they had to go to a revision office because some separatist enumerator took them off the voters' list.

The separatists changed the rules for the first time in Canadian electoral history: Would-be voters were forced to prove they were "domiciled" as opposed to "resident." The distinction was that domiciled people had to satisfy officials that they intended to live in Quebec permanently. If not, they were eliminated from the voters' list. This allowed the separatists to eliminate No voters such as students from other provinces who were attending anglo universities in Quebec as well as corporate transferees.

The Referendum Act, passed in 1978, also contained an unjust gag law, which effectively prevented individuals or businesses from placing ads at their own expense. They had to get approval from the Yes or No Committee to do so, and many were turned away. During the referendum I received a poignant letter from a well-heeled individual in Toronto who was upset when the No Committee rejected his offer to buy two full-page advertisements, one in a French daily and another in the *Gazette*, which would simply have stated that he wanted Quebec to remain part of Canada and admired the French language and culture.

It was another example of Liberal control over the political approach taken by the No Committee during the referendum, which in effect became a form of censorship and official impediment preventing communication from well-meaning Canadians outside Quebec.

I decided to publish a special supplement during the referendum, with a unique and very ambitious nation-wide poll as its centrepiece. I have always been a big fan of psychoanalyst Erik Erikson, who explored the neurosis of nations, and to me the diagnosis seemed to fit Canada. The country did not need a divorce. It needed a couch. And to help analyse the problem, our poll posed dozens of questions to

Quebecers and non-Quebecers. What did they like and dislike about one another? What did they like about Canada? How did they intend to vote?

The supplement also contained essays by prominent thinkers such as Mordecai Richler, William F. Buckley Jr., Peter Lougheed, Benoit Aubin, Conrad Black, and Northern Telecom chief Jean Monty. *Post* advertising reps only sold one advertisement, to the Canadian Legion in Quebec. Companies were frightened to take sides.

The *Post* poll and Quebec supplement was published on September 23 and made headlines and broadcasts coast to coast. Only 36 percent of Quebecers polled said they would vote Yes, 40 percent said No, and 24 percent were undecided. This was an unusually large undecided proportion and if past voting patterns held, five times as many undecideds would opt for No as Yes. This was only logical. Undecideds were by definition cautious folks and would avoid anything as risky as a Yes vote. Using that logic it looked like the referendum would reject separation 59 percent to 41 percent, or roughly the same outcome as in 1980.

Besides that, *Post* pollster Conrad Winn of Compas Inc. in Ottawa added a clever "tracking" poll that showed how soft the 36 percent declared Yes voters were. Yes support melted away when respondents were told that transfer payments would stop, passports would be refused, and other negatives.

This poll boded well for the federalist cause and days after its publication Prime Minister Jean Chrétien cavalierly said he was sleeping soundly at nights. Other polls showed that the Yes vote was sagging behind the No vote. That's when Bouchard took over the campaign and turned up the rhetoric. Just weeks later, Chrétien went on national television calling it a national crisis. The Liberals organized a gigantic unity rally in Quebec and some organizers claimed that 150,000 Canadians descended on downtown Montreal on October 27 to hear speeches in praise of the country. Naturally, the separatist media in Quebec downplayed the size of the crowd. One commentator placed the number at a paltry 30,000. A French newspaper estimated the size to be considerably less than 75,000. No one knows the exact figure but the variation in estimates was predictably partisan.

I flew to Montreal the day of the rally to interview Quebec's reclusive labour godfather, Louis Laberge. The meeting had been arranged through Fred Doucette, who had run Prime Minister Mulroney's office for a number of years. The meeting was held in the exquisite $2,500-a-day suite that Mulroney used to occupy when visiting Montreal while prime minister.

Its living room was stunning, large enough to accommodate a cocktail party of one hundred or so. The dining room sat twelve easily and the bedroom included an ensuite sauna. Laberge walked in donning a Yes pin. He brought a union pal and for three hours he gave his perspective on the Quebec situation.

Laberge and other union leaders had been in bed with the Parti Québécois for years. In return the separatists had supported pro-union legislation.

Of course, the marriage had not always been a happy one. The two parted company temporarily after the 1980 referendum when the Lévesque government took on the public sector unions to cut costs. The union leaders turned against the separatists and helped bounce them out of office at the next election.

Laberge was one of the most powerful men in the province, although few outside Quebec knew anything about him. He had recently retired as director of the Caisse de Dépôt et Placement du Quebec, the Quebec pension-fund manager, and as head of the Quebec Federation of Labour. Laberge had been a driving force behind the marriage between the unions and separatists.

Years before, in an interview after the 1980 referendum, he told me he had voted No. Now he was an avid separatist. That day he was totally unimpressed by the show of affection going on outside. Horns were honking and people were shouting outside the hotel all morning.

"It's very nice that English Canada says we love you, but this is too much today," Laberge said. "On the eve of a referendum all those people taking trains and planes and driving here should save their money and spend it on the sick and poor in their own provinces."

He said Ottawa's demonstration was too little too late. "I knew a guy once who went to jail for beating up his wife every time he had a drink, and each time she visited him in jail he told her sincerely that he loved her. His kind of love wasn't good enough."

To Laberge, Canada was a wife-beater and nothing could salvage the marriage. "I was not born a sovereigntist. The federal government made me a sovereigntist."

Laberge's involvement was key to understanding the strategy of the separatists. The referendum vote was to be equivalent to a strike mandate. It was not an outright vote to strike. This was a tried-and-true union technique, because once the mandate was obtained it represented a gun held to management's, or Ottawa's, head.

"A Yes vote in the referendum is like a strike vote. And we don't go to the boss ahead of time and say, are you prepared to negotiate with us, because he'd tell us to go to hell. But once we have a strike vote then the boss will negotiate with us."

Laberge said that a close No vote or Yes vote would still require Ottawa to negotiate a new arrangement with Quebec. He suggested that Prime Minister Jean Chrétien appoint an independent negotiating team, because he could not negotiate on behalf of English Canada.

"English Canada should do what Jacques Parizeau has done. And that is to appoint someone other than himself to undertake the negotiations. I don't want to tell English Canada who should be their chief negotiator. Like labour negotiations, I may not like the people on the bargaining committee for my boss, but it's his business who does the negotiations for him. The most important thing is that the bargaining committee will be the true representatives of the people. And Jean Chretién is not. That guy is an embarrassment."

The debt will not be a deal-breaker, added Laberge. "We have never denied the debt is there. And if you want us to pay 25 percent of the federal debt or 24 percent or 23 percent that will depend on how strong or weak your negotiators are. But for those who say we can't use the Canadian dollar, I will say if you want us to pay the debt we have to have money you will accept."

I asked Laberge what English Canada should do the day after a No vote.

"English Canada cannot assume there will not be another referendum. If there's a No vote, Canada must take the opportunity of sitting down with us to make the changes that should be made in order to avoid another referendum," he said.

Laberge's solutions were simplistic: eliminate Ottawa from all of those areas that the province now manages and stop meddling in attempts to shore up the French language and culture. He did not feel that a Yes vote would bring about a crisis on currency markets. "If you hide Chrétien the day after the referendum I think we will have no problem. Why should the market be so perturbed? Do you know how many new countries are created every year that are smaller than Quebec? There were nine new countries created this year.

"There was no referendum vote taking place in the U.S. recently when the yen pulled the U.S. dollar down, was there? The fears of a crisis are just the nonsense from big banks and big business."

Laberge discounted the results of the Cree referendum held days before the interview and its near-unanimous rejection of separation. "The Cree referendum has absolutely no effect. They don't give a hoot in hell about Canada or Quebec. Aboriginals want all the modern services but don't want to pay a bloody cent for them."

His xenophobia knew few bounds. He disliked money, aboriginals, and francophones who were not French. He said he was shocked that more than half of the Montreal children enrolled in French-language schools were not of French extraction. This was similar to Bouchard's hideous remark during the referendum that the problem with Quebec was that not enough white babies were being born. He later apologized for the remark.

The night of the referendum was nerve-racking. Results were frighteningly close and for one brief period the Yes vote overtook the No side. At that point, I asked our currency expert what was happening to the Canadian dollar in Tokyo and Sydney. "It's in a free fall," he replied.

A Yes victory would have meant a long night. Canada would likely have been involved in a full-blown currency crisis with the dollar collapsing. With nearly $2 billion of debt to roll over each week with foreign investors, the country would have probably had to be bailed out by Washington and the International Monetary Fund. Canada would have been another Mexico—which is why U.S. President Bill Clinton in a press conference days before the referendum uncharacteristically told Quebecers to vote No. Washington was worried.

At the end of a very long evening and a result that was thoroughly inconclusive because of the closeness, Parizeau blamed the defeat on "money" and "ethnics." That remark caused former Ontario premier Bob Rae to comment on television that Parizeau must have been drunk.

But Rae was naive to have never realized what Canada was dealing with. Parizeau was dead serious. This was simply English Canada's first glimpse of the racism and socialism of the separatists. Parizeau resigned the next day but never apologized.

A tired Chrétien declared victory, but it was hollow. An even bigger cloud loomed over the country than before. Chrétien's victory speech was clearly uninspired. Liberal backbenchers and others were furious, because they had been told by his handlers to butt out. The referendum was thought to be a cakewalk and the prime minister wanted all the credit.

The referendum made world headlines the next day. But Quebec remained in the news a second day because of Parizeau's resignation. American editorialists and cartoonists had a field day, harshly criticizing his racist remarks. In some papers, more ink was devoted to the story of Parizeau's departure than to the significance of the close vote. It was an international embarrassment.

Parizeau's speech wasn't the only scandal. News began to dribble out days after the vote about the high percentage of spoiled ballots in No areas. One friend reported that in her polling station, voters wearing Remembrance Day red poppies were forced to take them off because red was a Liberal colour. Lineups at francophone polling stations were short while anglophones and allophones at nearby stations waited, in some instances, up to three hours.

A class action lawsuit was filed on behalf of an untold number of anglos and immigrants denied the right to vote because they could not produce their provincial medical card on the day of the referendum. They argued that the card was never mentioned in government literature as being a requirement to vote. One of the victims was a Chinese Canadian, left off the list for not having a medical card even though he showed proof that he was a licensed doctor who had practised in Quebec for eleven years.

But the spoiled ballots revelations were shocking. In Laval, where the No side outvoted Yes two to one, a shocking 12 percent, nearly 5,000 votes, were rejected for trumped-up reasons such as applying too much pressure, or too little, when marking ballots. In this riding, as in other heavily anglophone and allophone ridings, the percentage of spoiled ballots significantly exceeded the province-wide spoiled ballot percentage of 1.8 percent.

About a week after the referendum, I called electoral office spokeswoman Lise Dellaire to find out how many people had been disallowed before the voting. How many had been reinstated? How many had been denied a chance to vote on referendum day?

She was abrupt and clearly annoyed at the questions. She said she had no figures on refusals, but gave me figures as to how many were added to enumeration lists and how many didn't vote who could have.

Some 51,207 double entries were stricken, as well as entries for students, transferred workers, hospitalized persons, and dead people. She said this was not an unusually high number. Among those stricken from the list was an immigrant doctor who provided the necessary documentation but could not vote because he was listed as six years of age. Polling officials were not allowed to correct it on the day of the referendum.

She told me that the initial enumeration listed 4,817,407 eligible voters. After two revisions, the tally came to 5,086,980, an increase of 269,573 voters. But considerably fewer voted. Or perhaps they did and weren't counted. The great unknown is whether ballots disappeared. Clearly, the referendum itself was turning into a scandal. The separatists had Mexicanized the process. Under pressure from the local media, Quebec's chief electoral officer, Pierre Côté, announced an examination of the ballots in three ridings. Only the losing, or Yes side, could demand an official recount and did not.

That was the first tipoff that something was seriously wrong. The province was stonewalling demands to have a complete recount. Why would it do this when the separatists had lost by a mere 52,000 votes unless they had something to hide? It turned out, I was to learn months later, they did.

5
Sedition

The spoiled ballot scandal was bad enough but then Equality's Andrew Male called on November 8 with even more disturbing information. A "communiqué" had been faxed to Quebec military personnel from Bouchard's Official Opposition office on October 26, trying to recruit them to join a Quebec army some time after a Yes victory. The separatists had tampered with the country's armed forces.

Defence Minister David Collenette's office confirmed the information and faxed me a copy. I got a copy of the Criminal Code and the communiqué appeared to be a case of sedition under Section 62 of the Code. Equality Party leader Keith Henderson thought the same and sent out a press release publicly condemning the communiqué as treasonous.

The next day, I suggested that Bouchard and the Bloc Québécois defence critic, Jean-Marc Jacob, appeared to have broken the law. That was bad enough, but even more odious was the fact that Bouchard had never told Quebecers that they intended to set up an army immediately after a Yes victory.

The communiqué's headline said "A Sovereign Quebec will have need of all Quebecers now serving in the Canadian Armed Forces, estimates Mr. Jean-Marc Jacob, MP for Charlesbourg."

Jacob was quoted throughout the communiqué. "Obviously, because of its financial constraints, Quebec should not aim to equip itself with an army capable of protecting the integrity of its immense territory. It is unrealistic. Quebec needs a defence force to watch over and intervene on its territory, to participate in foreign peace missions and to respond to local needs such as disasters or rescues," Jacob said.

"The MP for Charlesbourg believes that to properly carry out its functions, Quebec will have need of all Quebecers presently enlisted in the Armed Forces," said the release.

Then Jacob was quoted as saying: "The day after a Yes win Quebec should immediately create a Department of Defence, the embryo of a major state, and offer all Quebecers serving in the Canadian Forces the chance to integrate into the Quebec Forces while keeping their rank, seniority and retirement funds as a means to ensure a better transition."

The English version of the release was incorrectly translated and Jacob actually said "some time after a Yes win" not "the day after." That aside, the release said Quebec pays 23.5 percent of the Canadian military budget, or more than $2.6 billion a year. It would not spend more upon becoming sovereign and would save approximately $700 million since "Quebec will no longer have to pay for Canada's extravagances, buying too much for too high a price."

It was cleverly couched to get across a message from Bouchard and his Bloc without directly attributing the call to arms to Bouchard himself. Instead, it quoted Jacob who, if he chose to, could have distanced himself from the quotes or nitpicked about context.

The *Post*'s legal counsel agreed that the communiqué appeared to be seditious. "Every one who wilfully (a) interferes with, impairs or influences the loyalty or discipline of a member of a force, (b) publishes, edits, issues, circulates or distributes a writing that advises, counsels or urges insubordination, disloyalty, mutiny or refusal of duty by a member of a force, or (c) advises, counsels, urges or in any manner causes insubordination, disloyalty, mutiny or refusal of duty by a member of a force, is guilty of an indictable offence and liable to imprisonment for a term not exceeding five years," said Section 62(1).

Even more outrageous was information leaked by military sources that in the days leading up to the referendum military officials forbade the movement of equipment or personnel out of Quebec. This was also highly suspicious and worrisome. The former Mulroney defence minister, separatist Marcel Masse, shifted weaponry from military depots in March 1992 from Moncton, Ottawa, and Toronto to a gigantic $100-million facility in Montreal's east end. There were concerns raised in the press at the time but plans proceeded and the result was a disproportionate amount of weaponry inside Quebec.

The media virtually ignored the sedition angle. Was there a coup d'état being planned? Why else would Bouchard be enticing soldiers to defect? Was there a separatist chain of command already in place to organize the defectors? Was there a game plan regarding the weaponry? Had oaths of allegiance to Quebec been sought and obtained? How many separatists had infiltrated our armed forces? Were the top brass aware of such possibilities and if not, why not? Why wasn't Ottawa investigating the matter and pursuing charges?

Andrew Male then called to say that a former Equality Party candidate, Montreal lawyer Brent Tyler, had decided to convince a justice of the peace to lay private charges of sedition against Bouchard and Jacob.

In any other country, evidence of sedition would have sparked a political probe as well as a police, or security forces, investigation. Tampering with the military is a serious security matter.

Tyler, a handsome and fiery litigator from Drummondville, east of Montreal, took on the case because of government inaction. The law allowed that if he could convince a justice of the peace to lay charges, justice officials would have no choice but to pursue the matter. Such public-interest advocacy was nothing new to Tyler. He had taken on other such cases. In the spring of 1995, he convinced the United Nations Committee on Human Rights that Quebec's restrictions on school children, which denied the children of francophones or immigrants access to education in English-language schools, were unjust because this denial of their educational rights was based on the ethnicity of their parents. The UN ruling came out months before the referendum. A few of us wrote about it but it was another news non-event across the country and within Quebec.

"We must push this issue because it's so flagrant. It's shameful that Collenette and [Justice Minister Allan] Rock have not done something. What more do they need to know? This press release [urging Armed Forces to defect] was sent to every defence installation. They were planning a coup d'état and were caught at it so let's see whether Canadian law still applies in the province of Quebec," said Tyler.

Tyler's first attempt to get charges of sedition laid against Bouchard and Jacob on November 8 would be rebuffed by a Montreal justice of the peace, Louise Baribeau. "She wanted to string me along for weeks. But I told her, 'If it's going to take you weeks, at least receive the information.' She didn't want to and said she'd take weeks to decide."

Eventually, Tyler said he found out she shouldn't be involved because she personally knew Bouchard. Undaunted, Tyler then "swore his information" (made a formal legal complaint) to an associate chief justice named Céline Pelletier. Tyler explained that Pelletier said the original justice of the peace was still seized of the matter and that Pelletier "tried to put me off." But on November 13 he was able to swear his information before her. I recorded this good news the next day in a column and said this meant the courts were going to deal with this misbehaviour. But the day my column was published Tyler was called by the judge and asked to come to her courtroom the very next morning. The judge imposed a gag order, which meant that the press, and even members of the public, were forbidden to attend the proceedings. Publication bans go on all the time in Canada, but shouldn't in a free and open democracy, particularly since the hearing involved a matter of public interest and high-profile public figures.

The rest of the media ignored the story. On November 16 I was called by a producer from CBC Newsworld's show hosted by Don Newman. I know Don and assumed that his producer wanted to talk about Tyler's sedition case. Wrong. The producer said that they wanted to do a show about how the Reform and Tory parties were targeting the same donors for campaign contributions.

This was not news. The Liberals were also targeting the same donors; this is just the way the political process unfolds. I urged her to read the sedition column and Newman to consider that as his program's topic. They declined.

Tyler had been an Equality Party candidate in 1994. He grew up in Drummondville and was totally bilingual. His father was an immigrant from the United Kingdom and his mother a fifth-generation anglophone Quebecer. He was angry at what had happened to his province and to anglophones over the years and had been involved in civil rights lawsuits. He was also upset at what he saw as the abandonment of Quebec anglophones by the rest of Canada.

"There's all this talk about the Rest of Canada and what it does or does not want if separatists win the next referendum. But I'm a fifth-generation, bilingual Quebecer. I'm the Rest of Canada too. I'm not a separatist and Montrealers are not separatists. We voted No in large numbers. We're the Rest of Canada and who is our premier? Who is speaking on behalf of us? Why would our citizenship be negotiable and not yours?"

Like so many anglo activists, he had a few horror stories to tell.

"I came from rural Quebec and my dad wanted me to

go to French school, but the local parish priest said there was no way they could have a little Protestant in their school. So my family had to move fifty miles away so I could. Then to get into a French high school, my parents had to pay $1,000 because I was denied the right," he said.

"The kicker for me was when the province decided to take over the running of the schools. My mother was a school nurse at Richmond High School and a damn good one. She was told she had to speak French even though the students were English-speaking. She was given a deadline. She tried and failed. She was eventually fired. Here my mother had done a good job for umpteen years and she was eased out by discrimination.

"She went to her local MNA, who was a PQ, to complain and ask for clemency because of her years of experience," recalled Brent. "And he said, 'Madam, it's our turn now.' Remember she was an English nurse in an English school fired because she couldn't pass a French-language test."

Tyler had other bad experiences as the only anglophone in his French-language law school in Sherbrooke. "They ridiculed me, and the professors dished out all this crap about how evil the anglos were and had been and here my family had been victimized for years. It was all part of the game by the separatist intelligentsia in the media and academia: to propagate the culture of the victim and demonize anglos and the wealthy."

Tyler talked about his skirmish with the two Montreal judges and said he planned to take his case to a justice of the peace in Ottawa. He felt he'd get a fairer hearing. Besides, Bouchard had sent the fax out from Ottawa so if a crime had been committed, it had been committed in Ontario. The hearing was set at the end of November and I took off after Collenette and the military brass. Why weren't they looking into information that separatists were trying to obtain oaths of allegiance from sympathetic officers eager to set up a rival army? Wouldn't it be a good idea to ask everyone in the military to swear an oath of allegiance to Canada, in light of what appeared to be infiltration? Why wasn't there an internal probe into how much infiltration had occurred?

Indications of separatists in uniform surfaced. An incident had occurred after the Gulf War that was never publicized. A group of soldiers hoisted up the Fleur-de-lys flag in place of the Maple Leaf flag. Fighting ensued and seven went to hospital, said Scott Taylor, editor of the soldiers' magazine *Esprit de Corps*. Another brawl took place in Germany between loyal Canadian soldiers and separatist soldiers.

A spokesman in Collenette's office said the minister wouldn't comment because it was "before the courts," meaning Tyler's case. But that was a cop-out. Here was a private citizen doing what the federal government itself should have been doing and now the government was using that as an excuse. Instead, Tyler was forced to live off charity. Some donations were sent to me to help pay for his expenses. Like others engaged in the fight against separatists, Tyler and his family were sacrificing a great deal on a personal level.

"My wife is a Bolivian immigrant and she wants us to move out of Quebec. She's fed up with all this and doesn't think anything will change just as is the case in Latin America where she comes from. Meanwhile, I'm playing Captain Canada and we're going broke," said Tyler.

After the sedition columns, I got calls from two French-Canadian soldiers who said that separatists inside and outside the Canadian Armed Forces had been organizing a coup d'état. Brent had similar calls. One of the officers who called agreed to be quoted, but not by name because orders were not to talk to the press about the communiqué.

"Canadians don't realize how serious this is," said the soldier. "Don't we realize that the lunatic fringe of the separatist movement kidnapped and murdered in the 1960s? Don't we realize that for three decades they have infiltrated government, politics, and the media? Radio-Canada has been completely compromised. Of course they have infiltrated the military."

He also pointed out statements made by Bouchard during the referendum, unreported in English Canada, that after a Yes outcome Quebec intended to prevent Ottawa from moving out of the province any military weapons, equipment, or jet fighters. He added that another Parti Québécois member had boasted that "we have 14,000 soldiers in our military already."

Another soldier told me that French-Canadian soldiers thought to be sympathetic to the cause were asked if they would swear an oath of allegiance to Quebec, rather than to Canada.

"I cannot believe this has been ignored by the media except yourself. Peacekeepers in Bosnia were sent the communiqué. I lost sleep over what a Yes vote and defections by soldiers would have resulted in. You could've had serious conflict between those who remained loyal and those who did not. Consider the possibility. You are a Canadian officer the day after the base commander informs everyone that now that the referendum is won, we expect you to switch your allegiance. I wouldn't have followed him but we're talking potential for serious violence between soldiers. I'm a Canadian first and a French Canadian second. But there are separatists in the military. When I came out strongly for No, many of my French colleagues in the military call me a 'vendu', a sell-out."

He saw a link between the French prime minister Jacques Chirac's stated support for Quebec independence, days before the referendum, and Bouchard's tacit support for French atomic testing. Was France flexing its muscles to make it clear it would back an independence movement in the face of Canadian resistance?

"It's naive not to imagine conspiracies. History is conspiracies and the separatists have had a long time to plan this. Bouchard was in France as ambassador for a long time and knew all the players. They are ruthless. Look at the fraud during the referendum. One American soldier said to me, 'Was there cheating in the Quebec referendum? Are we going to have to have UN soldiers monitoring the next referendum, as the UN did in Nicaragua's last vote?'

"The big guys are covering their asses over Somalia but military lawyers are looking into this," he speculated. "But it's like Jack Nicholson in a movie once said, 'You want the truth? You can't handle the truth.' I think they're scared of what they'll find."

Shortly after those interviews were published, Tyler lost his case. The Ottawa justice of the peace described the communiqué as "a job offer."

"A job offer?" scoffed Tyler. "The step he jumped is that these people [soldiers] are already employed and have an oath of allegiance to the government of Canada. If that's the case does that mean that the U.S. government or any other government can make a job offer to our military to join them?

"It's not a job offer. It's an offer to desert. You cannot just say I quit and leave the military. The resignation has to be accepted. A series of steps must be taken. Bouchard drafted it like a job offer but they made a mistake and went too far. Their communiqué was inviting, inciting, encouraging a transfer of the loyalty of a member of the Canadian Armed Forces to a Quebec army."

That was bad enough, then a week or so later Tyler was told that the Ottawa justice's tape recorder did not record his proceedings, meaning there was no transcript of his evidence or the reasons for judgement. Then Tyler lined up a lawyer in Vancouver willing to take the appeal, only to have him back out weeks later.

It started to look like Brent's efforts would be to no avail, so two more strategies were launched. I contacted some friends in the RCMP and got the name of a member of the force's national security branch and laid a formal citizen's request for them to investigate. That set the ball in motion. Other Canadians did the same.

Even if Bouchard's communiqué was not quite sedition under the Criminal Code, which requires a difficult burden of proof such as intent and malice, it was certainly seditious in nature. It was also quite unbecoming that a member of Parliament would try to entice military personnel to defect to another army. In a subsequent interview, Collenette agreed. "One alternative to any judicial proceeding is if members of Parliament feel concerned about it, my party or the Reformers, they should bring it up."

There was a precedent. A royal commission appointed by Parliament in 1946 reported that MP Fred Rose, a Communist, gave the Russians details about a secret parliamentary session in 1944 and was a spy for the Soviets. Arrested on March 14, 1946, he automatically lost his seat in the House of Commons after being sentenced to six years in prison.

"I'm surprised that none of my colleagues in the House of Commons has raised this [Rose expulsion and probe], since it might be more appropriate to deal with it in that manner," commented the hypocritical Collenette.

He was saying that somebody else should do his dirty work. After all, he was the defence minister responsible for any military matters. He cooperated when called but refused to be put on the spot. But he hinted that a full-blown probe within the military might yield up some pretty frightening facts. Some 31 percent of the armed forces personnel were French and a good chunk were probably separatists.

"This is a very, very dangerous area," said Reform Party leader Preston Manning in a later interview. "The communiqué may not technically constitute sedition [under the Criminal Code] but it may be seditious or unacceptable behaviour. I said to Jacob, 'What if the day after a Yes vote you had military people showing up for duty?' That certainly would have meant that you had counselled a treasonous act and you would be guilty of treason. We must draw a line in the sand."

6

Breakfast at the Ritz

Brent Tyler had become for me one of those larger-than-life figures. His attempt to throw separatists in jail for sedition was admirable and interesting enough. We met for breakfast at the Ritz to talk about the case. But he brought up another angle that had not been suggested to English Canada: the partition of Quebec, which would allow No voters to remain Canadian.

"This country cannot negotiate away my birthright or those belonging to half the province who voted No in the referendum," he explained. "If Canada is divisible, then so is Quebec. So after the next vote, divide the province and let the separatist part of it leave but not the rest."

This essentially was what the Cree and Inuit had argued during the referendum. It was only logical. He elaborated, and described how the map could be redrawn based on the last outcome. The No vote was 67 percent in Montreal; 75 percent in the Ottawa Valley and around 90 percent in the aboriginal lands.

"If you look at the referendum returns, you can see the

outline of their country. It sort of extends from eastern Montreal to Quebec City," he said.

We joked about this tiny sausage-shaped country that Bouchard could end up with. Tyler said that the boundaries were actually very similar to those of the original Lower Canada drawn by the British. They were also similar to a separate country as suggested by Raymond Barbeau's book, *La Laurentie*. That book made a case for a separate French country. So did another book written later by anglophones Bill Shaw and Lionel Albert.

"You could not call it Quebec because I live in Quebec and Quebec is part of Canada," said Tyler. "It would have to be called something like Laurentia or Maisonneuve or Nouveau Quebec."

Partition was a brilliant idea and an incredible weapon to use against the separatists. It would drive them crazy because tiny little Laurentia, with dairy farms and civil servants in Quebec City, was not viable economically. Partition called their bluff using their own logic. Canada was not divided over the issue of separatism. Quebec was.

Not only was partition a knife to hold to Bouchard's throat, as separatism had been held to English Canada's for three decades, but partition was possibly a sensible policy if a critical mass of diehard separatists existed in the Yes regions. This is simply what David Ben Gurion argued about the Palestinians in Israel: that they should be given a homeland if all else failed. In Canada's case, I believed, if all else failed to keep the country together and stop the separatist damage, then giving separatists the Yes region of the province made perfect sense. But this would only happen, of course, if an amendment to the constitution permitted it to happen.

My next column exposed the continuing favouritism by Ottawa towards Quebec separatists. This particular example was significant and showed how the separatists kept pushing their luck and getting away with murder due to federal fear of creating a fuss. In November 1995 the federal health minister had begun imposing a monthly $420,000 fine against Alberta, for violating the Canada Health Act involving cost cuts in a handful of clinics. Meanwhile, Quebec had been violating the act in a much more significant way for years without consequences. After the referendum, Parizeau escalated this unacceptable behaviour. One of the intentions of the health act had been to ensure that Canadians had portability with their medical care. So if an Albertan had a heart attack in Montreal, the act required that his province would reimburse Quebec health authorities for doctors' fees and other costs related to the Albertan's illness while in Montreal. This included reimbursement for hospital care as well as drugs.

But Quebec had got away with refusing to co-operate and share costs. This meant if a Quebecer had a heart attack in Calgary, Quebec refused to give Alberta full reimbursement for doctors' fees incurred. This was in contravention of the act and yet nothing had been done about it by the Mulroney or Chrétien governments. The excuse given by Quebec was that its doctors were the lowest-paid physicians in Canada and Quebec could not pay higher doctors' fees for services provided to Quebecers anywhere else in the rest of Canada. The result is that the out-of-province doctor and his hospital absorbed the difference.

Interestingly, Manitoba and Newfoundland also pay their doctors substantially less than Alberta or Ontario but those provinces never pulled this stunt. They reimbursed other provinces for whatever doctors' fees their residents rang up while visiting.

After the referendum and while still premier, Parizeau announced that Quebec would not pay full hospital costs either. This was another example as to how separatists flouted the laws of the land and were not taken to task.

"A special border agreement to defray costs was set up between Quebec and the Ottawa region, but over the years doctors have submitted bills and simply not been paid," wrote Ottawa doctor Charles Shaver. "The Ottawa General Hospital, for example, has had to swallow huge costs for fees."

At the end of November, I flew to Montreal to do a taping of the Public Broadcasting System's "The Editors." Also on the panel was separatist mother superior Lise Bissonnette, editor/publisher of the separatist *Le Devoir*, and Joan Fraser, editor of the Montreal *Gazette*. I had been a regular on the show for months and was eager to debate the post-referendum situation with both Fraser and Bissonnette.

Fraser is a prudish woman and says very little of substance on television. Neither has her newspaper done much to defend its anglo readership and their rights over the years, with the exception of William Johnson. In fact, the *Gazette* is chief cheerleader of what Johnson has dubbed "the lamb lobby," those naive, well-intentioned appeasers who have encouraged the federal government to let the separatists get away with murder for thirty years.

Bissonnette and Fraser are equally humourless. Bissonnette makes her points with the long-suffering manner of a Dominican nun. She's thoroughly closed-minded. Fraser equivocates.

"The Editors" is a free-for-all of journalists, with a moderator who throws out questions to get things going. Several programs are taped at a time at the gorgeous but decayed St. Stephen's Club in Montreal. This was a fitting venue, because the club had declined as the anglos left a decaying Montreal economy.

The program's panel that day discussed Montreal's deterioration. Bissonnette actually said that separatism had very little to do with the city's economic problems. Fraser said nothing. But I couldn't resist.

"When I immigrated to this country in 1966 from the United States, the New York City, the financial capital, of this country was Montreal. And twenty years of linguistic discrimination against anglophones and allophones has ruined that. It is responsible for the departure of 330,000 persons and 1,400 head offices and you know that."

The facts were truly grim and ideologues like Bissonnette would not admit it. Departures began in 1974 after the

Liberals stabbed the anglos in the back and the floodgates opened after 1976 when the separatists triumphed.

By 1996, Montreal was still in decline. Housing starts had declined for eight years and in 1995 were the lowest since 1965, when Canada Mortgage and Housing Corp. began keeping statistics. One out of every five Montrealers was on social assistance because job growth in two decades had averaged only 12 percent compared with 30 percent in Toronto and 50 percent in Vancouver. And what job creation had taken place was also suspicious. For instance, in 1994, 20.9 percent of Quebec's workforce was employed in the public sector or by government business enterprises. By comparison, only 17 percent of B.C.'s and 18 percent of Alberta's workforces were public sector. Besides, Quebec's brightest sector, aerospace, had been heavily subsidized by federal grants, defence contracts, and provincial handouts.

All in all, Montreal fared the worst among the thirty cities in the U.S. and Canada that have more than two million residents. Montreal had the highest unemployment, most poverty, lowest job creation record, and lowest per capita income of the thirty urban centres. As a bone to anglophones in that beleaguered city, the newly anointed Premier Lucien Bouchard created a new cabinet position called the minister for Montreal, designed to kickstart the city's flagging economy.

By coincidence, around this time I had decided to interview the Toronto-based mining financier Seymour Schulich, because he was about to give to York University in Toronto the country's largest single donation, a $15 million gift to its business school. During our luncheon interview I found out he was a former Montrealer who had left for political reasons. So in my column I pointed this out: here was one of the country's richest men, who left because separatists treated him badly with the result that he did not give the gift to his alma mater, McGill University, but to York instead. This was because he severed ties, emotionally and otherwise, after the separatists took over the province's agenda.

"Leaving Montreal was the direct result of the election of René Lévesque," he said. "I was working at [Montreal money manager] Beutel Goodman with Austin Beutel, Ned Goodman, David Williams. We had a meeting right after the election and no one spoke in favour of staying. We moved, and the four of us have done an enormous amount of business in Toronto. I would guess that we have generated as much as $500 million in economic benefits in Toronto, and that's being conservative."

Next I wrote a column suggesting that Canadians insist on the partition of Quebec if the population was divided after the next referendum. Those living in regions that voted No had just as much right to remain in Canada as someone living in Vancouver or Toronto. The next referendum would be about partitioning Quebec, not about wresting it away from the rest of Canada. Aboriginal lands were not leaving Canada either and their residents voted overwhelmingly to remain Canadians. So they weren't going to be negotiable, nor were their lands. Likewise the Ottawa Valley and Montreal would leave. The next referendum should be evaluated on a regional basis. English Canada would have to give permission for any portion of Quebec to negotiate to leave. Only those ridings where there was overwhelming support to leave could negotiate with Ottawa and the provinces. "Partition is the Quebec nationalist's worst nightmare, making Quebec independence nearly impossible, practically speaking. Discussing partition provokes tantrums from Quebec nationalist politicians and media," said Stephen Scott.

He also suggested that before any changes to Quebec's boundaries were considered, any such discussions would have to first be approved by all Canadians in a national referendum.

A group calling itself the Preparatory Committee for the Partition of Quebec was formed and published an insightful manifesto: "[Separatist legislation in Quebec] denies the right of [Quebec] federalists to opt for the same choice. It presumes that by simply stating that the present boundaries of the province are inviolable, this would be accepted by the rest of Canada and by the federalist regions of Quebec. They know that their case is very weak."

The group, comprising anglophone Quebecers, had been lobbying fiercely for support. Fortunately, it convinced the Reform Party to include partition in its national policy platform, the only party to do so officially. By contrast, the Quebec Liberal Party stated in its constitution that Quebec was not divisible but Canada was. This was identical to the stance taken by the separatists.

Reform's policy was very clear. It would require any Quebec referendum to be conducted on a regional basis so that those portions of the province that chose to remain in Canada could do so. Partition was the most practical solution. Indications were that only 25 percent of Quebec's population could be termed die-hard secessionists. Partition would allow those people and their messiah, Bouchard, to form their own little homeland without abrogating the rights to citizenship enjoyed by the other 75 percent of Quebecers.

Partition would mean that francophone separatists living in Montreal who didn't want to be Canadians could move to Laurentia and become Laurentians. And Laurentians who wanted to remain Canadians could move to Quebec.

It was ironic that the Reform Party had the best policy position concerning Quebec even though it had virtually no presence or support from anglophones in Quebec. In December 1995 the party issued two more policy papers outlining their position: Quebecers who left would have to pay their proportion of the debt; Quebecers who left would have no passport or citizenship privileges in Canada, no control over currency or monetary policy, and no automatic participation in existing trade or other treaties. Quebec's borders would be negotiated keeping in mind aboriginal protection and the requirement that there be a land bridge to the Maritimes. Best of all, Reformers favoured the partition of Quebec to protect the rights of those voting No.

Preston Manning noted in an interview in December 1995: "We're doing what the prime minister should have done at the outset of the referendum. Federalists will never go into another referendum as ill-prepared as they were on October 30 and Quebecers will never again be so misinformed as to the costs of separation."

In answer to that sensible policy, Canada's bumbling prime minister announced more measures to appease the separatists. He tabled legislation to give Quebec "distinct society" status as well as a special veto over constitutional amendments. It was another appeasement stroke, giving in to the never-ending demands of separatists while handing over control of the governance of the country to regimes in Quebec set on destroying it.

Quebec's media jumped all over the notion of partition put forward in my column. Even *Post* columnists attacked it, along with the usual politically correct suspects such as the *Globe*'s Jeff Simpson. But grassroots movements began springing up all over Quebec in support of the idea. One of the most aggressive was run by a Montreal businessman named Mark Kotler.

Kotler had given up on unity and had become an anglo separatist. He favoured partition now, whereas Tyler and the Equality Party supported partition only if all else failed.

Kotler felt that francophone secessionists would eventually succeed. So he wanted Ottawa to allow the formation of a new province, called Nouveau Quebec, to be created comprising those regions and cities where the majority wished to remain Canadian. Kotler wanted the boundaries of this new province defined by plebiscite before Lucien Bouchard's next referendum. Convinced the secessionists had a critical mass, he formed the Citizens' Committee for a New Province in a bid to remove anglos from being held hostage.

"There is no charge for joining. If we need money to do things we will ask members for donations at a later date. But we are all volunteering our time and I'm paying for all costs. And the response is great. We can't keep up with the calls and I have three people here helping me," said Kotler.

Like so many, Kotler became politically active after the referendum and Parizeau's racist speech.

"I said I have to do something after he insulted me and others by calling us ethnics," explained the fifty-two-year-old father of three. "The feeling among all the people here, without exception, is that Quebec will eventually separate. It could be one year or ten years from now. But they will. You can't deny constant bickering of two million people plus. As long as they don't have their state, they'll cause trouble in Canada. This is costing investment in Canada and Quebec."

Kotler said Canadians living in Quebec had only three options to choose from. "Option one is the federal government option that we have a unified Canada coast to coast. This is impossible because the Parti Québécois has only one motive, to secede. There is nothing the federal government can do to please Quebec. The second option is if Canada is divisible, so is Quebec. That somehow the province is partitioned after the Parti Québécois wins and Quebec secedes. The only problem is once they secede from Canada they're in the driver's seat and partitioning would not be allowed. The third option is our committee. We want to put a plebiscite up prior to the next referendum so the powers can realize they're not going to get whatever they want.

"There's 20 percent to 30 percent hard-core nationalists in Quebec and you can never appease a nationalist. They want their piece of land. And I understand that and I feel they deserve that. We'll help them get it. But they must respect our desire to remain Canadian.

"Montreal with 67 percent No stays in Nouveau Quebec. So do the Eastern Townships, south shore, land south to the U.S. and west to Ontario, Ottawa, and the aboriginal lands. When the rest of the population realizes what would happen without Montreal, a lot will decide to stay within Canada," he added.

"But if they don't, both Canada and the independent

region, the Republic of Quebec, can stabilize and return to establishing sound government for their citizens. The Province of Nouveau Quebec can take an active part in the growth of Canada. That's what our committee stands for."

I devoted an entire column to Kotler and his group, even printing his outfit's fax and telephone numbers. He was deluged with calls. A week or so later, he was invited onto Peter Gzowski's "Morningside" show and referred to me as "Saint Francis." I received flowers from two readers for publicizing the partition issue.

The point was that Kotler made more sense than anyone else had. If a critical mass had been reached, then divorce was essential. Besides, his idea of a plebiscite before the next referendum would put Bouchard and his bunch completely on the defensive.

The strategy shifted to publicizing the heroic efforts of Quebecers like Kotler who hadn't given up the fight. Guy Bertrand, the former separatist who waged the court battle against declarations of independence, agreed to an interview. I profiled him in *Maclean's* in December 1995 with the headline "The ex-separatist who wants to save Canada." In it, I described Guy's affiliation with the Parti Québécois. He had run for its leadership in 1985 after quitting the independence struggle in November 1994. He said he realized that Quebec already enjoyed a "de facto sovereignty-association" within Canada, and that independence was unnecessary and too risky to pursue. That's why he took the referendum laws and his old party to court. He felt that only the courts, not politicians in Ottawa, could save the day.

Since that legal battle, Bertrand had been shunned by and alienated from friends and family. His separatist brother, Péquiste caucus leader Rosaire Bertrand, had not talked to him since, but Guy remained more than ever convinced that the separatists were wrong.

"It's impossible to be more sovereign if we separate than we are now. Why? Because we are sovereign within the constitution, de facto on language, culture, with the civil code, with our distinct institutions, and no one is attacking our language," he said in a telephone interview with me. "What Mr. Bouchard was proposing, the partnership, was to have the same things we have in common with the rest of the country already, like passports, currency, the Queen. So why separate? It's about a symbolic seat in the United Nations and a national anthem. That's no reason to separate. It's crazy. If it was impossible to keep our French language and identity and culture, that would justify leaving, but that is not the case."

The unfair treatment of the anglophone minority in Quebec also bothered Bertrand and there would be a mass, disastrous exodus if the separatists succeeded. "I'm not sure many English-speaking people would have stayed in Quebec after a declaration of independence. We lost 170,000 between 1976 and 1980. How many would leave Quebec if we separate? A poll in March [1995] said that a minimum of 500,000 would leave Quebec and possibly one million," he said. "The anglophone minority was here in 1760, almost as long as we were. It is totally unjust to run them out."

Bertrand decided after the referendum to take his case all the way to the Supreme Court of Canada to establish that any vote on independence without a prior amendment to the Constitution would be illegal.

"I left the Parti because I opened my eyes. We were fanatics, always thinking we were right. I felt that we could not impose our old constitutional quarrels on the next generation. I realized that the separatist option was not good for the Quebec society. When they decided to have a new referendum, I asked to see Parizeau. He refused. So I wrote to him and told him that this option would cause permanent damage to the Canadian and Quebec societies, and I couldn't defend it any more. I decided we cannot pass our whole life trying to separate. We must learn how to live together."

Bertrand said he had studied other democracies and determined that Canada with the constitution was a model society just as it was. "I started reading about federalism in other countries like Switzerland, the United States, and

Australia. I found out that we had the best federalism in the world, most decentralized. I think twenty-five years from now people around the world will find out that this federalism we have, a de facto sovereignty-association, is the model.

"This country is only a little child, just 123 years old. Children make mistakes. We cannot destroy a country because we have some administrative problems, such as power over immigration, communications, or manpower traning. We're not going to destroy a country for that. That's ridiculous."

Bertrand, like most of us, was fed up with the federalists' mishandling of the separatist threat. "Now, the citizens should take in their hands this responsibility to protect this country because the politicians have not. During the the campaign, the Liberals didn't talk about the illegality of trying to separate unilaterally even though my case was victorious. No one talked about that. When you have a government not defending the constitution or protecting the Charter of Rights and the rule of law, that's the end. That's what the government is there for. The Charter of Rights is the most important thing in this country."

As Bertrand said, the rule of law was Canada's most important cornerstone, and the bench, rather than the ballot box, looked like the best hope for the nation.

Just after Christmas, Tyler called on behalf of the Special Committee. They wanted to hoist partition onto the national agenda and planned a rally at McGill University on Sunday, January 21. I was to be their lead-off speaker. I said I would cancel plans to spend a weekend in New York City, but only if the rally was going to be large. This would be the only way to attract the national media and get partition onto the national agenda. It would be a waste of time talking to just one or two hundred people.

In early January 1996, Tyler reported that they were sure they could attract as many as seven hundred people. That was enough for me to call CTV anchor Lloyd Robertson and others to lobby them for national coverage. They obliged, as did others, and the rally marked a turning point in the battle against the separatists.

7
The Turning Point

Montreal was bleak on the day of the McGill rally and bracing for a snowstorm. All the speakers and organizers met ahead of time to have dinner and discuss the rally's format at the Moby Dick Restaurant, at Maison Alcan, Sherbrooke Street. This restaurant was on the fringes of the McGill campus and a busy watering hole where Equality members gathered to discuss politics most Friday nights. Brent Tyler greeted everyone at the door and explained the rally's format. I was to speak first, Guy Bertrand last. There were nine speakers in all and everyone would be given ten minutes and no more.

The rally was to start at 7:30 p.m. Some speakers were nervous. Every one had been waging a battle of some kind against the separatists. Besides Bertrand and myself, Stephen Scott, Keith Henderson, and William Johnson were on the roster.

Johnson and his wife arrived from Ottawa, where he covered national as well as Quebec politics for the Montreal *Gazette*. A fluently bilingual ex-Jesuit, Johnson told me there was a good chance that he would be fired by the *Gazette* for participating. I pooh-poohed it, unable to believe that the *Gazette*'s editor Joan Fraser would be that foolish. Fraser was gunning for him, others said, because she disliked his tough-minded columns. They were not the Liberal "lamb lobby" party line that she so totally toed. Before the rally on January 10, Fraser told Johnson that his full-time job would be terminated as of April 30, one week after he reached the age of sixty-five. He continued to write just one column per week for the *Gazette* until then and on May 3 wrote his first column for me in the *Financial Post*. While it might seem reasonable to retire someone at sixty-five, facts are that rules are bent for columnists as popular as Johnson. She wasn't about to bend rules for William Johnson.

The dinner was my first face-to-face meeting with Guy Bertrand, whom I had interviewed over the telephone. Tall, thin, and elegantly tailored, he looked positively regal. With his jet-black hair, dark eyes, and prominent nose, he looked like a Mohawk warrior chief. His voice was mellow and deep. He spoke slowly and deliberately. He sat beside me to talk and thanked me for the articles about him.

I suggested that he speak first instead of me, not last. This was because some of the speakers might be boring and the audience, and television cameras, might give up by the time he was to speak. Surprisingly, he responded: "When I speak they will be standing on their feet."

Dinner lasted ninety minutes or so and the conversation was lively and political. Everyone had a laugh at the expense of *La Presse* editor Alain Dubuc. He had written a column that day for the *Toronto Star* that described the event as ridiculous and all of us as "weirdos." An anglo commentator on the CBC in Montreal had also been contemptuous. This was good because such advance publicity would draw a bigger crowd.

Tyler asked us to pose in the Alcan atrium for a commemorative photograph before heading out into the snowy night. The trek was cold and uphill to McGill's Moot Court building. What a way to spend a Sunday night, but it all became worth while. Several television trucks were parked in front of the building. The rally would get coverage and partition get an airing.

The building was jammed and the floor was dangerously slippery from wet snow traipsed in by the crowd. Organizers were trying to direct people to classrooms with teleprompters for the overflow crowd. Television camera crews and reporters with notebooks were scurrying about getting quotes. Some people had brought their own lawn chairs. One woman was angry because she could not get into the Moot Court room where we would speak. The room had filled an hour before and held roughly four hundred.

We were directed up a back stairwell to a classroom. Coffee and juice were available, coats and hats were heaped on a table. Guy Bertrand was badgered as he made his way to the makeshift waiting room. He came over and told me he had changed his mind after talking with me. He would be the sixth, not ninth, speaker.

He told a revealing story. He had been constitutional adviser to René Lévesque and just before the 1980 referendum he suggested that the Parti Québécois could simply declare unilateral independence and see what happened next. René Lévesque said that would be illegal and unconstitutional. "We could not do that."

Lévesque believed in democracy but Parizeau and Bouchard do not, he added. Tyler and I urged him to tell the crowd outside that anecdote. He did.

At 7:30, we filed into the Moot Court. There was barely enough room to walk down the steeply banked aisle because people were sitting on the steps. People were standing in the back. Three men at the back waved and shouted, "Lady Di." Partitionist Mark Kotler came up to shake my hand and said, "Hi, Saint Francis." This was a far cry from the last time I had spoken publicly in Montreal and was pilloried by my journalistic peers.

If the best revenge was to be success, it came in spades.

In all, an impressive 1,200 Montrealers turned out and an estimated seven hundred more had to be turned away. Television coverage was substantial. The entire two-hour event was carried by a French television network.

My speech was short and sweet. I said I was an "ethnic" or immigrant from the United States who did not think there was anything wrong with Canada, only with our politicians and their reluctance to uphold the constitution. I talked about how Ottawa had ignored the rule of law, about the shenanigans that took place during the referendum, about seditious behaviour by Bouchard, about partition.

Throughout the rest of the speeches, most of which were in French, the crowd was enthusiastic, cheering wildly and clapping often. They were motivated despite years of pummelling by the separatists and their Liberal accomplices. Partition gave No voters hope and it was to become Lucien Bouchard's worst nightmare.

The reviews in the press the next day were predictable. The French newspapers grudgingly admitted the crowd size was impressive but discounted the event's importance. A *Gazette* columnist wrote a vicious and inaccurate piece the next day. He said most of the speeches were in English and that "Diane Francis fled early to the safety of Toronto." The facts were that most of the speeches were in French and that I had to leave to catch a plane because of a speaking engagement in Toronto the next morning.

The event was an undeniable triumph and made a difference. That was because Prime Minister Chrétien watched it on French television. He had been unable to sleep due to jet lag after a trip to Asia. The arguments about the rule of law and partition sank in. He called William Johnson after the rally to personally tell him so.

Two days after the rally, federal Justice Minister Allan Rock for the first time in thirty years talked about violations of the law in Quebec and said his department might get involved in some of the court cases under way.

Then two days after that bombshell, Chrétien's constitutional deputy, Stéphane Dion, talked about the possibility of partition, repeating the logic: "If Canada is divisible then so is Quebec." The separatists were apoplectic and the Quebec press went into a frenzy. Two days after Dion's partition statement, Bouchard was sworn in as premier. And at a press conference that followed, he totally lost his cool concerning the partition issue. He said Quebec was not divisible but Canada was because "Canada was not a real country."

That infuriated English Canada. Normally sanguine editorialists blasted him with both barrels. Open-line radio show hosts across the country had a field day. On the Monday after the rally, the prime minister jumped onto the partition bandwagon. Trudeau did the same five days later.

The separatists brought out their biggest guns to try to refute or destroy partition as a possibility. But it was too late. The issue was on the national agenda. Canadians outside Quebec embraced the concept. Michael Brown, president of Ventures West in Vancouver, wrote saying that partition would solve the problem of the division of the national debt. He pointed out that the federal debt per capita was roughly the same as the total Quebec provincial debt per capita. Partition would mean that probably half of Quebec's population, the 49.6 percent Yes vote, would form a new country and would be free to repudiate their share of Canada's debt. The other half, the No vote, would stay in Canada and would be free to repudiate their share of the Quebec debt. So No voters would have exactly the same debt burden as Yes voters after partition took place.

Others began realizing that partition would avert, not cause, violence because no Quebecer would be forced to live in a jurisdiction against his or her will.

Another *Post* reader, Clark Muirhead, pointed out that partitioning in Canada had already successfully occurred. He suggested a three-way partition of Quebec: federalist, aboriginal, and separatist. "There is a precedent for dividing the province. Back when Canada was a British colony, it became clear that its two factions were not getting along.

With the Constitutional Act of 1791 it was decided to divide the colony into Upper Canada and Lower Canada, English and French, Protestant and Catholic. It reduced the problem for decades.

"If carried out with justice and fairness it could politically stabilize our country for generations to come. It may be painful in the short term. Proper steps will have to be taken to minimize any pain."

The province and country were buzzing with new ideas. Partition was in play. A newspaper poll in Quebec showed that 78 percent of anglophones and 41 percent of francophones supported it. Now was the time to find other angles to pursue to keep the separatists on the defensive.

8
Lunch at the Ritz

I flew to Montreal on February 1 to meet Andrew Male, Keith Henderson, and Brent Tyler. For nearly five hours in the Ritz's bar we debated and discussed a range of issues and initiatives over lunch. As we sat in a corner of the posh bar, several other patrons came over to thank me for my columns and participation in the McGill rally. Significantly, Henderson, Male, and Tyler were ignored, even by people who knew who they were. But they deserved more recognition than anyone because of the amount of time and effort each had dedicated to the cause.

For years these three, along with Stephen Scott, Neil Cameron, and others, had been the only "opposition party" in the province even though by 1994 they did not have a single seat in the National Assembly. The Liberals, both provincially and federally, were part of the problem. So were Mulroney and his Quebec "Tories."

It was obvious that the Equality Party had got little credit for its work. For hours, they told me about the dirty tricks, censorship, and media malpractice that had nearly destroyed the party. It could not pay any of its workers and was reduced to being supported by two businessmen, Bill Sullivan and Alan Singer.

"The Liberal Party in Quebec is another separatist party," said Tyler. "We call them the Plan B federalists. They just want to go a little more slowly than the Parti Québécois."

They even had their suspicions about the way the Liberals, Tories, and businessmen on the No Committee waged the campaign.

"I think they realized that a huge victory for Canada would remove the enemy or straw man, separatism, that they needed. So they purposely eased up to make it a closer outcome," suggested Tyler. "They shut out our efforts and others. About halfway through the referendum the No Committee suddenly did nothing. I think they were point shaving by doing nothing. Then at the last minute they realized that they might lose and panicked."

What Tyler and the others were saying was that the Liberals and Tories had used the separatists to win elections. Put another way, if the separatists had been badly beaten in the referendum, the Parti Québécois would have probably abandoned separatism as it had after the last referendum and become another socialist/labour party like the New Democrats. But that would not have been desirable for the Liberals with their Quebec leader, or the Tories with theirs. For nearly three decades, national parties had had mostly Quebecers as leaders in order to appeal to voters inside and outside Quebec who wanted to fix the separatist problem. If the separatist problem were to be solved, then a Quebecer would not have to be leader, said Henderson.

This explained why, for the third year in a row, federal Liberal Party whip Don Boudria in Ottawa personally sat in on all inaugural committee meetings at the beginning of each calendar year in order to ensure that Bloc Québécois, not Reform Party members, were elected as vice-chairpersons. It was a dangerous game. Chrétien needed the Bloc Québécois as Her Majesty's Official Opposition so he could pose as Captain Canada. This tactic clearly suited the separatist-leaning Quebec branch of his own party.

The Tories had been no better. Their Quebec leader, Jean Charest, could have challenged Bouchard and his Bloc as official opposition after the 1993 federal election merely by joining forces, in coalition, with the Reform Party. The Tories' two seats would have given the combined conservative parties the same number of seats as Bouchard had (54 MPs). Such a tie must be put to a vote or adjudicated by the House Speaker. That coalition could have then put fiscal restraints and other issues, not separatism, at the top of the national agenda. Then, in 1994, a Bloc MP died and a Liberal was elected in his place, which would have allowed a Charest/Reform coalition to easily become the Official Opposition. Again Charest, like every other Quebec national party leader, needed a separatist threat to be elected in English Canada and to be elected by federalists inside Quebec.

"The untold story is how much the Liberals have been infiltrated by the separatists in Quebec," said Male. "It's a scandal and they have been the ones giving bad advice to Chrétien."

Mulroney's behaviour had been more egregious. He made a pact with the devil itself and put separatists in his cabinet, Bouchard and Marcel Masse. The quid pro quo was for him to muck around with the constitution again in order to give Quebec more than it deserved. Canadians were told that the constitution had to be changed because Quebec had not signed it. But Quebec had not signed it because the separatists were in power and wouldn't sign it. The only thing wrong constitutionally with Canada was that prime ministers from Quebec were too frightened or ambitious to uphold the constitution.

The fact that Mulroney had twice failed to pull off a new constitutional deal had allowed Parizeau to get the issue reinstated in the Parti Québécois platform and to regain power provincially. Despite the obvious failure of such behaviour, Chrétien was running around to English Canada and trying to shove down the country's throat "distinct society" and special privileges for Quebec.

The Equality Party wanted Ottawa to stand up to the separatists. Some of its supporters had been in the Freedom of Choice movement that sprang up in the 1970s to combat language and educational restrictions. The party was formed in 1989 and captured four seats that same year and more than half of the anglophone vote where it ran candidates.

Then a series of embarrassments struck; three of its members left the fold or tried to join the Liberals. This was partly due to the fact that new political parties attract the types of candidates that others would find unacceptable. But desertions also had to do with the dirty tricks played by the Liberals and the media.

"The party was virtually murdered when CFCF-TV's news director issued a memo in May 1993 to stop covering us," Henderson said over lunch that day. "The news director wrote that Equality was a fringe player and was getting too much coverage. But a virtual blackout followed." The inevitable result was that the Equality dropped calamitously to 1 percent from 6 percent in the opinion polls. (Those polls were province-wide, by the way, and Equality had substantial support in anglophone ridings.)

Leaked the memo by a CFCF reporter upset about censorship, Henderson wrote back to the news director: "As head of Pulse News, the Montreal English community's chief source of news, you may feel that too much attention has been devoted to the policies and activities of the Equality Party. We received 4.69 percent of the popular vote in 1989, some 160,000 votes, a strong majority of English-speakers. The six-percent figure in recent polls suggests we may do even better next time around."

Similarly, English-language CBC radio and television commentators and anchors were indifferent or downright rude, as was the largest anglophone private sector station, CJAD. The Montreal *Gazette* abandoned coverage during the 1994 election and sent a reporter to Equality headquarters on the very last day of the campaign. Only a weekly, the *Suburban*, carried news and commentary in favour of, and about, Equality Party issues and candidates.

"There has been a virtual blackout wherever possible by the media or sabotage when coverage of Equality was required," said Christy McCormick, the *Suburban*'s feisty editor, who has championed the cause on behalf of Montreal's anglophones, unlike the *Gazette*.

Equality was dealt an illegal blow in the 1994 provincial election when a consortium of Quebec television networks denied Equality the chance to participate in the leadership debate. Only Liberal leader Daniel Johnson and Parti Québécois leader Jacques Parizeau would be invited, and the debates were to be in French only.

This flew in the face of Quebec's Election Act, which required broadcasters to give free, fair air time to leaders from "parties represented in the national assembly or which obtained at least three per cent of the valid votes at the last general election." Equality qualified on both counts.

Henderson wrote to the television consortium and the Canadian Radio-television and Telecommunications Commission, reminding the CRTC of its policy circular No. 334, which says: "The broadcaster does not enjoy the position of a benevolent censor who is able to give the public only what it 'should' know. Nor is it the broadcaster's role to decide in advance which candidates are 'worthy' of broadcast time." The guideline urges broadcasters to provide, among other things, "equitable" political coverage.

If the same restrictions had been applied during the 1993 federal election, Canadians would have been unable to hear Preston Manning and Lucien Bouchard debate. Even worse, protested Henderson, those debates would have had to be held in English only. The commission and consortium held firm, citing a subsequent court decision in Ontario that overruled the policy circular and allowed TV networks the latitude to choose who could participate in televised debates.

Then the party was frozen out of the referendum debate by the Liberals. Under the Quebec referendum rules, Yes and No committees were established and given the power to vet all advertising pertinent to the vote. They were also given one dollar per voter, or about $5 million, to spend on the campaign.

"We made application to be an affiliated group to Daniel Johnson's No Committee [including Tory leader Jean Charest] and had to go to court to be recognized as having the right to advance ideas that the Quebec Liberals would not advance," explained Tyler. "For example, we wanted to point out you cannot have a 50 percent-plus-one vote that authorizes a unilateral declaration of independence where only 25 percent of the Canadian population is called upon to vote.

"We wanted to tell voters that Guy Bertrand had won a court case that made the separatists' plans to secede illegal. They refused to allow us to speak our piece and didn't want constitutional and legal arguments. We lost three weeks of a four-week campaign fighting it out in court. We won, then they offered us $2,500 to run some kind of campaign. By that time and with that amount, it was too late."

A healthy democracy should pave the way for the dissemination of many opinions and freedoms. What happened to the Equality Party raised questions about Quebec's, and Canada's, commitment to an open society. It also raised questions about the Liberals.

More Liberal dirty tricks had been taking place after the referendum.

A resident of Campbell's Bay outside Ottawa, Faye Stafford, had crossed swords with a Liberal and was fuming. After the referendum, she became involved with a tiny grassroots group called the United Quebec Federalists. Their strategy was to circulate petitions among residents to pressure municipal councils to endorse a simple resolution: "This municipality affirms and secures its Canadian status as being part of one Canada, indivisible."

Stafford organized the petition drive for the Pontiac

County district. The purpose of the resolution was to stand up to the separatists. In essence, the organization was trying to get their local government to state that they would never have to leave Canada. The reason for this resolution was that few, if any, Quebec No voters felt protected by the Liberals. After all, it was the party that had agreed to the removal of their linguistic rights over the years.

By February 1996, most of Pontiac's twenty municipalities had passed this resolution. This was hardly surprising since about 90 percent of Pontiac's residents voted No in the referendum. But in January 1996, Stafford's own municipality rejected the motion by four votes to two at the urging of its "Liberal" mayor. This despite the fact that she got signatures of support from more than half her community's eligible voters. Even worse, the Liberal mayor, Denis Larivière, organized a campaign to undo the resolutions already passed.

"I'm English and French and my blood is boiling and these Liberals are telling me to put my life in their hands," said Stafford. "I have done that for years and in 1995 my country almost went down the drain. These people are wolves in sheep's clothing."

She suspected that these politicians were playing it safe in case the separatists pulled it off.

I asked the mayor why he would oppose such a symbolic gesture of unity and loyalty to Canada. "First of all, a lot of people have gotten very carried away with the issue. We were not rejecting the part of the motion that said we were remaining part of Canada. My council rejected the first part of the motion that said the council assures people their Canadian status. My council has no legal right to do so and let's not lead people on and give them false assurances. I got a legal opinion."

Stafford got one too, from a constitutional expert. Mayor Larivière's was from a local lawyer. So if the wording was wrong why didn't the mayor help the group come up with acceptable wording? Or why not pass the portion of the resolution that wasn't a legal problem?

"I was elected to represent the people of Campbell's Bay and to manage the municipalities under the municipal code," he replied. "This effort is going to divide the county. There were two francophone municipalities not approached."

Stafford said she only approached the municipality she lived in, as was the case in others. She said it was up to locals to organize themselves and she could not be accused of not approaching some because she didn't approach any other than her own.

As for accusations of dividing the populace, Stafford said: "Divided? Ninety per cent of Pontiac County voted No. We have been accused of driving a wedge between the English and the French with the petition to keep Canada together. That's a lie. We have both English and French signing the petition.

"It's one thing to fight Lucien Bouchard, but at least he has the guts to stand up and be blunt about where he stands. These people tell us they are federalists but they are part of the problem."

This was just another example of Liberal mishandling. Another was Chrétien's damaging "distinct society" legislation after the referendum.

"It is being painted as harmless. It is an astounding resolution," wrote Marguerite Ritchie, president of the non-profit, private Human Rights Institute of Canada and former lawyer with the federal justice department. "It requires the House of Commons to take the distinct society into account in everything it does and it 'encouraged' all parts of the federal government to do the same."

The prime minister "has abandoned his loyalty to this country," adds the civil rights expert. "[It means] your Parliament and the government and public service you pay are now instructed that their concern is for Quebec and no one else."

Reform Party leader Preston Manning suggested three amendments: one that stated clearly that the resolution did not extend new powers to Quebec; another that stated that the government would protect the rights and freedoms of all Quebec residents; and a third that recognized Canada as one nation.

Chrétien and his Liberals defeated those three amendments. That meant the Liberals were willing to extend new powers to Quebec, to abandon protection of rights and freedoms of Quebec residents, and to reject the recognition of Canada as one nation.

The Liberals initially refused requests by Guy Bertrand before finally helping in May 1996. They never agreed to help a similar challenge by Stephen Scott. Quebec Liberals have tried to stand in the way.

"Chrétien had ample power to prevent the referendum, by disallowing the legislation, but he treated it as perfectly legal. He could have gone to the courts, but he did not. When private individuals [Guy Bertrand and his Citizens for a Democratic Nation] won a decision that the Quebec legislation was illegal, Mr. Chrétien closed his ears," wrote Ritchie.

Bertrand had also been shocked at Chrétien's unwillingness to uphold the law of the land against separatists and help him with his court case.

"To think that our federal government did not get involved in setting a precedent to protect all of us is unbelievable, truly unbelievable," added Bertrand in an interview in the spring of 1996. "What is wrong with them? You never see people in the streets of Quebec shouting for independence. Why not realize that a handful of people are causing all this trouble and it is not the will of Quebecers, francophone or anglophone?"

More glimpses of separatist leanings in the "Liberal" camp kept cropping up during the referendum. A Parti Québécois organization calling itself RESPEQ asked prominent people to sign a letter asking Quebecers to recognize a Yes victory as a valid democratic decision. The letter also appealed for respect, solidarity, and responsibility, in the name of the economy and job creation. One who signed was Liberal MNA for Outremont Gérald Tremblay, former Bourassa cabinet minister who worked on the No side of the campaign.

After the referendum Chrétien's cabinet shuffle made the separatists look like they were on a roll. Instead of ignoring the vote and conducting business as usual, Chrétien gave in to the separatists by offering "distinct society" and by shuffling his entire cabinet. Chrétien named seven Quebecers as cabinet ministers out of a total of twenty-five. That meant 28 percent of the cabinet was from Quebec while only 10 percent of the 177 Liberal seats were from Quebec. By comparison, Ontario provided 55 percent of the Liberals' power base in terms of seats and had only ten ministers, or 40 percent of the total. Chrétien also pushed out anglophone Quebecers and replaced them with francophones. Chrétien was sending an unintended message to separatists and their supporters: Keep on pushing us around and we'll give Quebec more than its fair share of cabinet seats and other privileges. Meanwhile, Chrétien's unintended message to anglophone Quebecers was: You're on your own.

In his shuffle, Chrétien even dumped Liberal MP and anglophone Shirley Maheu from her riding to clear a path for the election of francophone Stéphane Dion. In an interview in February 1996 she expressed her surprise. A local newspaper asked her if she jumped or was pushed. "Well, it hasn't been the result of any decision I've made, let's put it that way."

At the time, renegade Liberal MP Warren Allmand pointed out in an interview that the shuffle also removed Mount Royal MP Sheila Finestone from cabinet, representing the first time anglo-Quebecers had been shut out of the national executive since Confederation. Paul Martin Jr. technically had a seat in Montreal but his roots were in Ontario.

Lines between Liberals and separatists in Quebec blurred even more during and after the referendum. Even after Chrétien and Dion endorsed partition in January, Chrétien cabinet appointee Pierre Pettigrew was even quoted as saying that if Quebec separated he would stay with Quebec. Even Mr. Partition, Chrétien's other new cabinet member Stéphane Dion, was quoted during his by-election bid in March 1996 as saying that the separatist's Bill 101 in 1978 was a great piece of legislation. This was the law that sparked the exodus of hundreds of thousands of anglophones and removed Montreal as the country's pre-eminent business capital, and he admired it.

The Liberals had always been ready, willing, and able to stab their anglophone supporters in the proverbial back. For instance, in January 1996 they treacherously betrayed high-profile Montreal surgeon Dr. Roopnarine Singh. He had organized the city's annual Canada Day parade for seventeen years. He found when he went to city hall to get his annual Canada Day parade permit, as he had done every year, that he could not. The federal Liberals had swiped his permit because they wanted to organize the Canada Day parade in 1996. They wanted to stage-manage patriotism and avert what promised to be a highly charged event.

"I was speechless when the city told me we couldn't get our permit because it was already given to some government committee," he said. "I went public, and twenty-four hours later Sheila Copps backed down and declared the parade would be run by me again. They set up a committee to run it and I have agreed to cooperate with this committee even though it rankled me that the committee initially justified taking the parade away because they said we did not have the stature before the people of Quebec to pull it off."

The committee was wrong. Singh's parade last year pulled a crowd of 100,000. Just what did it mean by its "stature" remark? Singh became another victim of his own federal government.

On April 12, 1996, Singh announced his new political party, to be called the Bloc Canadien. Its principal plank was to partition Montreal off from the rest of Quebec so it could remain part of Canada. "The Bloc Canadien platform is that Montreal should be recognized as a distinct society, bilingual, multicultural, and free. We also believe that Montreal has a right to determine its destiny and should not be a pawn or a hostage held by the secessionists," explained Singh in an interview.

"We believe these three things are needed to rescue the economy of Montreal.

"The only way to save the city is to remove the separation cloud overhead and that's what the Bloc Canadien will stand for. Partition of Quebec if Canada is partitioned. French Canadians are as loyal as English Canadians. It's just that you have a substantial separatist minority, 8 percent of the people, and they want to impose their will on the rest of Canada. Eight percent cannot impose their will on 92 percent of the people," Singh stated emphatically.

It was all head-scratching stuff. Just what was going on here? Had the Liberals been infiltrated by separatists? Were they stupid? Had they made a deal with the devil as Mulroney had? Were they just well-meaning appeasers who didn't know they should play hard ball? Were they in cahoots? Or was this about blackmail?

Then, in April, a Montreal reporter found an old article that Bouchard had written in 1961 while he was a second-year law student at Laval University. It provided an insight into what Quebec's political elite, federalist and separatist, had been up to for thirty years.

"I'm not saying that the realization of the Laurentian ideal [creation of a separatist state] would be a good thing: that's not where the debate lies, at least not in the current analysis," wrote Bouchard back in 1961.

"Put simply, the fact that some French-Canadians are trying to take Quebec out of Confederation could very well prove beneficial to all of us. It doesn't really matter if they succeed or not. What matters is that an attempt is being made.

"Without realizing it, separatists are in the process of putting into practice the 'brink of war' doctrine espoused by John Foster Dulles. Demands being made cause tensions, which will probably lead English-Canadians to grant certain concessions.

"They're fond of Quebec, our co-nationals. Don't ever forget it. They know very well that Canada without Quebec would no longer be Canada. Therefore, they'll do everything in their power to keep us in Confederation. Everything, including making concessions. Not so much out of love as out of self-interest."

The reporter who had found this article then called Bouchard to ask him if he was still playing that game. Bouchard stated that he no longer felt the same way but smiled and chuckled when shown a copy of his article. His coquettish response, of course, could also be part of the game. To play brinkmanship correctly, you must flatly deny that it is a game, or else your opponent may be emboldened enough to call your bluff. On the other hand, hinting that the game may be under way encourages the appeasers to meet demands because they are made to believe that eventually the game players will stop short of independence.

Trudeau had this game figured out and he described it as "blackmail," not brinkmanship. In an article he wrote in 1950 in the first issue of *Cité Libre*, he said: "The country can't exist without us [Quebec], we think to ourselves. So watch out you don't hurt our feelings...We depend on our power of blackmail in order to face the future...We are getting to be a sleazy bunch of blackmailers."

Then in 1992, on the eve of the Charlottetown Accord referendum, Trudeau warned Canadians not to fall for it. "In today's Quebec, the official blackmail refrain gets back-up from a whole choir of those who like to think they are thinking people: 'If English Canada won't accept Quebec's traditional, minimum demands, we'll leave...' Leave for where? What for?"

The blackmailers' game is to keep increasing the amount of ransom demanded. Ransom, in the separatists' case, was for Ottawa to give away special privileges and to turn a blind eye to constitutional abuses against the anglophone minority.

Of course, the only way to stop the blackmail game was to refuse to pay any ransom. But in the absence of this counter-strategy, the separatists just kept getting bolder and bolder. In French this is known as *étapism* or the step-by-step destruction of foes. And Canada was their enemy.

9
Drinks at Moby Dick's

In early March, another gathering was held at Moby Dick's with Equality's Andrew Male, Keith Henderson, Neil Cameron, Brent Tyler, and other activists such as teacher Don Donderi and his American wife, Verna. The couple had worked for years helping the Equality Party and had made headlines when they erected a highway sign on one of Quebec's borders, which quoted Bourassa after he invoked the notwithstanding clause. It was a takeoff on a statement made by Bourassa: "Welcome to Quebec, 'where we have suspended fundamental human rights.'"

Neil Cameron came for a drink. I asked him about the declining enrolment in his college and other anglophone educational institutions as the separatist policies of the Liberals and Parti Québécois continued to deny anglos the opportunity to work for governments or even the private sector. He said the situation had worsened.

"The exodus between 1973 before the Liberals' Bill 22 and 1979 was not only a stick, but a carrot situation. There were lots of jobs out west. During this time, my students were the traditional anglophones, WASPs, and Jews," he said. "Now my students are immigrants' children and they are all baffled by this. Their parents are usually lower middle class and vulnerable to globalization. They don't have much confidence in themselves and they see jobs leaving. Hitachi and Volkswagen both left Quebec last summer and there is a continuing deterioration of the economy and it will get worse."

Cameron, a historian, said the French were not systematically oppressed by the English.

"French Canadians were more oppressed by their own institutions than by anglos. The French priests in the Catholic Church ran the province. French politicians ran the provincial government. There has only been one anglo premier of Quebec and that was in the very beginning of Confederation."

The British had given Canada self-government out of fear that the swollen American army, after the U.S. Civil War, might try to enlist the help of the French to invade Canada. So concessions were made and in 1867, with Confederation, the English and French languages were given constitutional protection in the federal Parliament, the federal courts, the Quebec legislature and Quebec courts, but not elsewhere in Canada. The separatists, with the help of Quebec Liberals, dismantled protections for English inside Quebec, beginning in the 1970s at the same time that Prime Minister Trudeau was ensuring protection for French outside Quebec, and for English inside Quebec, through bilingualism legislation as well as through eventual constitutional and charter protections.

Added Male, "The British allowed French-Canadian Catholics to be elected to Parliament seventy years before Catholics were allowed to be elected in the British Isles."

Such rights to representation predated Confederation. The British, in 1791, gave self-government and a legislature to Upper Canada and to Lower Canada. Unfortunately, even though the majority of Lower Canada's residents were

French, there was no protection for their language and there was actually a debate in Lower Canada's assembly as to whether French could be used. It was, as a matter of practice, but its ironclad protection did not come about until Confederation in 1867, according to William Johnson.

When the Industrial Revolution came along, francophone workers may have been exploited, but so were Irish, Jewish, and other anglo workers. Besides that, francophone industrialists did their share of exploiting workers too. As for the absence of francophones in management positions, Cameron pointed out that this had to do with the difference in value systems among the ethnic groups. The best and brightest English kids in Quebec went into business while the brightest French kids in Quebec went into the professions, the priesthood, or politics. This reflected itself in wages.

As William Johnson wrote in his book, *A Canadian Myth*, "A study by Jac-André Boulet, published in February 1979, found that among male workers in Montreal, the income gap of 51 percent in favour of anglophones in 1961 had decreased to 30 percent by 1971 and to 15 percent by 1977. At this rate, Boulet predicted, the income gap would disappear altogether by 1982."

The facts are that anglophones are clearly disadvantaged and that this reality is cleverly hidden. For instance, statistics in 1985 showed that a unilingual anglophone earned 23.4 percent more than a unilingual francophone. That was widely reported in Quebec. But when parroted in the *Toronto Star*, in a column in 1992 that criticized anglophone Quebecers for "whining" about their problems, Montreal journalist Peter Sauve took the matter to the Ontario Press Council. A year later, he won his case. "Missing was the fact that English-speaking Quebecers as a group are more highly educated than francophones," said a *Star* story printed in 1993 about the fact that the press council upheld Sauve's complaint against the *Star*. "He [Sauve] also said the column was misleading because it missed out another important statistic showing that a unilingual anglophone earned 12.8 percent less than a unilingual francophone with the same education."

Sauve quite rightly said to the press council: "How could the columnist, who got his earlier numbers from the same chart, have missed that key figure?"

He also wanted to know why the *Star* had not printed his letter to the editor designed to add the vital information that was missing in the column. It was separatist propaganda, designed to discredit the case against linguistic discrimination.

Such media malpractice is widespread inside Quebec among francophone journalists who use facts selectively and publish propaganda.

The past had also not been without discrimination against francophones. Certain clubs excluded francophones as members and there were stories about francophones being refused service in stores if they did not speak English to clerks. But mostly these were anecdotal. Besides, Jews were also excluded from certain clubs and some had been the victims of anti-semitism by francophones and others.

But the mythologies continued, propagated in textbooks as well as in the political arena, according to Johnson and others. In June 1996 Bloc Québécois member of Parliament Suzanne Tremblay introduced a bill that would overturn Louis Riel's treason conviction in 1885. The Métis leader was hanged. "Tremblay said then prime minister John A. Macdonald had Riel tried in Regina instead of Winnipeg to ensure there would be only Protestant anglophones on the jury to ensure a guilty verdict," said the Canadian Press story. "'Louis Riel was hanged because he was a Métis, because he was a francophone, because he had come to the defence of a distinct society,' Tremblay said."

Such nonsense was either madness or, more likely, mischief. After all, such a bill would put the appeasement-oriented Liberals, with huge representation outside Quebec, in a very awkward position. It was simply another example of the time wasted in Parliament over Quebec issues and the constant, tiresome dredging up of ancient history without any relevance to today's Canada.

Whatever happened to Riel was a matter for historians to determine, not Parliament. As for the other discriminatory actions, these were over long ago and certainly could not justify the recent abuses against the anglophones that had been allowed to occur with impunity since the 1970s, he added. Leaders were just frightened of losing elections or of having to deal with the violent elements in the separatist camp.

The economic damage to Quebec as a result of separatist policies and discrimination against anglophones continued to be serious, wrote Montreal venture capitalist Pierre Arbour in a controversial book in 1993 called *Quebec Inc. and the Temptation of State Capitalism*. Arbour worked for the cornerstone of the separatist scheme, the Caisse de Dépôt et Placements du Quebec, as a key portfolio manager. A francophone, he created a sensation because he debunked the myth that state capitalism or linguistic restrictions in Quebec have benefited anyone.

"The temptation of state intervention is a temptation every government has had," Arbour said in an interview with me in early 1993. For example, he cited the Alberta government's involvement with Novatel Communications Ltd.; British Columbia's with British Columbia Resources Investment Corp.; the federal government's with Petro-Canada; and Ontario's with the Urban Transportation Development Corp.

As for Quebec, "The real losers are not the rich, not the anonymous private investors in the market, but the whole population of Quebec, passive and captive to events decided without their approval. All Quebecers, as unwilling shareholders, emerged poorer from these adventures."

Arbour also dealt with another taboo. "I give my reflections on another kind of state intervention, the linguistic laws whose constraining clutch is, together with high taxation, partially responsible for the relative impoverishment of Quebec at a time when we are at a critical stage of our development as a francophone community."

Arbour left the Caisse and became a successful entrepreneur, involved in a number of venture-capital projects such as oil and gas limited partnerships in Western Canada; the privatization of Tijuana Airport in Mexico; and financing for cable television systems. He took months off to write his book because of his concern about governments and the mishandling of funds.

Arbour said the Caisse, which manages the $15-billion Quebec Pension Plan plus about $35 billion more in pension and insurance funds, had not made the return that it could have made. "The Caisse is supposed to have made 11.7 percent return. That's their figure. But I believe it could have made 1 percent more," he says.

(Of course, it's important to point out here that the Quebec Pension Plan has done significantly better than the Canada Pension Plan, whose funds are automatically loaned back to provinces in the form of bonds.)

As for Quebec, Arbour said most of what Parti Québécois leader Jacques Parizeau initiated, and the Liberals, too, has been a flop. About the only successes were government-owned monopolies Gaz Metropolitain and Hydro-Quebec, in his opinion. Others would differ on the issue of Hydro-Quebec, which many feel is bloated and over-exposed to US dollar debt, and has indulged in questionable accounting games.

Arbour estimated the Quebec Stock Savings Plan scheme cost Quebec's treasury $1 billion from 1979 to 1985. High rollers could write off 100 percent of their investments in new Quebec companies and 25 percent in existing ones. "The big winners were the accountants, lawyers, and brokers— not the public," he said.

Other basket cases include Sidbec, Dosco, Asbestos Corp., Quebecair, Petromont, and Davies Shipbuilding, which he described as "a living nightmare." Arbour said the Steinberg Inc. saga cost the Caisse $448 million in losses, because it would not allow the sale of the grocery chain to an Ontario outfit. The Brascade-Noranda Mines Ltd. losses by 1993 had reached $858 million and Domtar losses $117 million, plus lost interest.

Then there were the unknown costs resulting from unfair language policies and high taxation rates to pay for state interventions. As Arbour said, unfair language laws cost Montreal its pre-eminence as Canada's head-office capital. In a sub-chapter he called simply "Exodus," he had a chart showing the net outflow of 252,300 anglophones between 1966 and 1986. He then described how Quebec governments passively sat by despite this economic "haemorrhage."

"It is still possible for Quebec to act by making a fundamental change in its language laws to make them compatible with the Charter of Rights and Freedoms and to modify its tax levels to allow us to be more competitive, to become a more attractive place to transact business than we have recently been, compared to our Canadian, American, and Mexican neighbors."

For instance, Quebec's share of Canada's Gross Domestic Product, or sum total of all goods and services generated, had declined since the early 1970s from more than 25 percent of the total to 23 percent. This was due to the fact that throughout that time Quebec's economic growth had lagged behind Canada's. More recently, Canada's economy grew by 2.6 percent in 1993, by 4.2 percent in 1994, and by 2 percent in 1995. Estimated 1996 growth was also 2 percent, according to an April 1996 reported titled *Economic Outlook—Quebec*, published by the Investment Dealers Association of Canada. By contrast, Quebec grew by 2.4 percent in 1993, 3.6 percent in 1994, 1.8 percent in 1995, and an estimated 1.5 percent in 1996. If you compare the four-year Canadian average with the four-year Quebec average, Quebec's economic growth average from 1993 to 1996 was estimated to be 10 percent lower than the country's as a whole.

Quebec's economic growth represents $23,662 per person per year compared to Alberta's $31,422, Ontario's $28,483, British Columbia's $27,999, and even Saskatchewan's

$23,682. Only Manitoba and the Maritimes had lower incomes. The Investment Dealers' *Economic Outlook* applauded Premier Bouchard's announced balanced-budget goal, but added that huge economic constraints would make it difficult to reach that goal before 1999. This meant that Quebec lagged behind other provincial governments. By 1996, seven provinces posted surpluses.

Quebec's current economic sluggishness would be aggravated by outright independence, maintained businessmen such as Northern Telecom's Jean Monty and the Bank of Montreal's chairman, Matthew Barrett, in speeches and statements they made after the referendum. A debt crisis, and possible currency crisis, would ensue. Studies by prominent think-tanks and economists agreed.

"What arrangements would Canada and Quebec use for handling the debt? This issue might prove the most difficult of all. Assume that Quebec's share of the debt was determined to be 25 percent of the total, or approximately $135 billion to $150 billion. Even if Quebec were willing to assume responsibility for this debt, it could not simply be assigned immediately by Canada to Quebec. Authorization of creditors would be required and they would almost certainly insist on the payment of a substantial premium as compensation for the additional risk they would be assuming," wrote Patrick Monahan in the January 10, 1995, C.D. Howe Institute commentary entitled *Cooler Heads Shall Prevail: Assessing the Costs and Consequences of Quebec Separation.*

"This Commentary argues that the Canadian government would likely challenge a Quebec unilateral declaration of independence, at huge cost to Canadians in all parts of the country," wrote Monahan, associate professor at Osgoode Hall Law School, York University, in Toronto. "Section 35(1) of the Constitution Act, 1982, requires the Canadian government to act as a 'fiduciary' or a trustee on behalf of aboriginal peoples in Quebec. Before this trust relationship can be severed, the Canadian government must obtain the consent of the aboriginal peoples residing in the province who would most certainly oppose a Quebec unilateral declaration of independence. In fact, aboriginal groups would be able to argue that section 35 (a) obliges the Canadian goverment to oppose and contest a Quebec unilateral declaration of independence without their consent."

While legal wrangling worked its way through domestic and international courts, economic catastrophe would result as investors and lenders shied away from the mounting confusion around the question of who was going to be on the hook for the country's, and Quebec's, enormous debts.

In his May 1995 Fraser Institute Forum, Fraser analyst Robin Richardson described an independent Quebec as the most indebted industrialized country in the world. Among "true costs" of separation would be an increase of as much as 31.9 percent in overall taxes to pay debt-servicing costs, simply to maintain the same level of services and benefits as are now enjoyed by Quebecers and to balance a new government's budget.

"An independent Quebec would find great difficulty borrowing what it needs without a substantial further increase in interest-rate levels," he added. "A final potential consequence of Quebec leaving the Canadian Confederation may be an unwillingness of foreign and domestic investors to lend money, not only to Quebec, but also to the rest of Canada. The negotiations leading to separation would dispel whatever illusion may have existed on the part of investors in Canadian and Quebec government bonds as to the severity of the debt burden facing Canadians and Quebecers, and the impossibility of servicing this debt at existing interest rate levels, while maintaining government services, without unprecedented tax increases and/or further borrowing."

Quebec would also find trade relations difficult after separation, particularly so after a unilateral declaration of independence. Another C.D. Howe commentary in March 1995 by one of its policy analysts, Daniel Schwanen, concluded that the Quebec market is less important for the rest of

Canada than the reverse. This means that the confrontation and strong-arm demands of past separatist regimes would likely result in troublesome trading relations or even outright boycotts against goods and services. This would likely force many exporters to leave the province and set up operations in U.S. or English-Canadian markets rather than export from a troubled independent Quebec. It would also hurt the rest of Canada because it sells more goods and services to Quebec than to Japan and Europe combined.

But once the dust settled after a split, Quebec would face even more problems, because despite Parizeau's pledge to use the Canadian dollar it would likely be stuck with its own currency, according to C.D. Howe analyst William Robson in a March 1995 commentary. "Even the easiest transition imaginable would involve some awkward situation," he wrote. Banks, governments, and businesses would not be able to withstand a massive flight of capital but "it appears certain that secession will be accompanied by some movements of capital out of Quebec. So the rest of Canada and Quebec might want to put some special measures in place to reduce the chance that the initial shifts of credit and deposits will snowball into a panic that buries the union. Unless both turn their attention to the preservation of the currency union in the event that Quebec secedes, it seems an independent Quebec will mean an independent currency."

Little wonder that by 1995 all commercial and industrial leases plus some employment contracts signed in Quebec routinely contained "sovereignty out" clauses, nullifying the lease terms or, in the case of employees, triggering a payout or defrayment of the cost of a transfer to another part of Canada.

Such increasingly dire consequences as a result of the separatist cloud hanging over the country obviously converted Premier Bouchard into a born-again Ralph Klein deficit-cutter by spring 1996. His hope was to smooth the departure path and to prove to Quebecers that his government could improve the province's economy. But the task was daunting, if not impossible, given the disinvestment and avoidance of the province by investors following the referendum.

Besides, a Yes outcome or separation would spark a triple whammy, said Toronto-based francophone Claude Lamoureux in an interview with me during the referendum. Quebec would suffer from a further brain drain of francophones as well as anglophones, an even more severe loss of economic activity and a threat to the French language itself. Lamoureux, an actuary, was head of the country's second largest pension fund—the gigantic Ontario Teachers Pension Plan Board with $38 billion in assets compared to the Caisse de Dépôt et Placement du Quebec with $50 billion. I wrote a column about our lunch/interview and Lamoureux was, as always, very outspoken.

"To Yes voters I would say, 'Do you realize after this famous referendum you're going to have to do business in English?'" he said. "All the top business people in the world speak English."

He added, "Do they think they can divorce the same people that the next day they want to remarry with a different contract? Once divorced, what's the incentive for the other side to fix the problems? Can someone explain that to me?"

If Quebec left, he added that he would retain his Canadian passport and forgo a Quebec one because "a Canadian passport is worth much more."

What's worse is that a Yes outcome will cause even more head offices to leave Quebec and possibly even Canada.

"Many would do like the Royal Bank . . . really move your head office without admitting it. Once companies start moving out of Montreal they may just go to the U.S. where the weather and tax rates are nicer and the market is closer and personnel recruiting easier. This would not be good for Quebec or for Canada," he added.

As Lamoureux and others pointed out, the dislocation and disinvestment was bad enough already, because of the threat of separatism. But that night at Moby Dick's Brent

Tyler handed me and others copies of a newsletter that noted that even more destabilization was about to harm Quebec's economy. The newsletter had been published by an extremist group in February 1996 and was called *La Tempête* or the *Tempest*. The author was Raymond Villeneuve, a former FLQ terrorist and a Parti Québécois member. After the referendum, Villeneuve started an organization he called the Mouvement de Liberation Nationale du Quebec.

Villeneuve had been convicted of manslaughter in the bombing death of a security guard. He was eventually sentenced to twelve years' imprisonment, but fled to Cuba while out on bail awaiting sentencing. Unfortunately he returned, finished his sentence, and (with other FLQ pals including convicted murderer and kidnapper Paul Rose) became involved in the separatist cause again. Paul Rose had become leader of the Quebec branch of the New Democratic Party and preached his Marxist-separatist philosophy in schools, town halls, and elsewhere. The New Democrats said they did not endorse him and his NDP was not the real McCoy, but he took the name of the party in vain anyway.

Villeneuve's new Mouvement was much more frightening. Its inaugural meeting in November 1995 was attended by two hundred people, who heard Villeneuve describe No voters as "enemies" of Quebec. A news story in the *Suburban* reported that another convicted terrorist who attended that meeting suggested that someone should buy explosives to sabotage a company that had displayed English-only ads in the subway.

It seemed to the group at Moby Dick's that night that the separatists were escalating their warfare. The newsletter contained a "hit list" of twenty-two companies and fourteen individuals, including myself. We were described as "enemies" of Quebec who were to be driven out of the province. It was scary stuff.

"I don't think they are violent any more, but this guy did go to jail for killing someone and he's a real nut bar," said Brent Tyler, another listed "enemy" of Quebec.

Andrew Male told the group he had heard Villeneuve on an open-line radio show in Montreal. He was asked whether he was recruiting members for the patriotic militia he claimed was needed. "The host asked Villeneuve if he had any volunteers for his militia. He said he didn't have any or need any for the moment. But he said if anybody opposed separation or tried to partition Quebec it would be an act of war against Quebecers."

Some individuals on the list had already received death threats, such as Tyler. On the front page of the newsletter was Dr. Roopnarine Singh, the immigrant surgeon and Canada Day parade organizer. Also set up for special "punishment" was a cartoonist named Anthony Bonaparte. In the newsletter a couple of paragraphs were devoted to describing Bonaparte's "crimes." He had drawn a series of vicious cartoons caricaturizing Bouchard and Parizeau. The item was boxed for emphasis and contained Bonaparte's residential address and home telephone number. I filed this away for future column material and made a note to get in touch with Singh and Bonaparte at some later date.

It appeared that the separatists were turning the screws more and more tightly on "ethnics" and "money." Because of Villeneuve's history of violence, I brought the newsletter to the attention of my publisher and legal counsel. We had it translated and our security consultants took it to local police to explore whether I could lay charges against Villeneuve for threats or under the Hate Propaganda portion of the Criminal Code. A planned public appearance in Montreal was cancelled, just in case.

Some days later, *Suburban* editor Christy McCormick called to caution me against jumping to conclusions that the terrorists were back in business or that threats were to be taken seriously. "I wasn't there the night you were shown the newsletter, but I think some people around the table were pretty paranoid about what might really happen. I don't think these guys are violent," he said.

But he couldn't guarantee that, nor could anyone.

Besides, the Mouvement's newsletter was outrageous. Just who did these goons think they were? It meticulously named each company's chief executive officer and published their addresses, fax numbers, and phone numbers. Beneath most of the twenty-two companies' names was a quote that Villeneuve cited as proof that these companies were somehow "enemies." The quotes had come from speeches or internal memos.

Andrew Male then faxed me a copy of an article in the *Suburban* that reported that a company, Matrox Electronic Systems Inc. in Dorval, had received a threat. The result was it had warned employees about the danger and decided to boost security. The company had received a communiqué purporting to be from a cell of the FLQ on February 20 and it called the proprietor "responsible for the villainy of influencing the vote in the last referendum." The reference was to the fact that Matrox's president stated before the October referendum that any future expansion of the company's operations would have to be outside Quebec if the Yes side won.

Suddenly, I remembered that Matrox was one of the twenty-two companies on the "hit list." So I decided to call a few up on a random basis to see if they had also got threats.

Joel Segal, head of successful exporter Peerless Clothing Inc., said he got a letter that he promptly "sent off to the RCMP." His "crime" had been the fact that during the referendum he sent a memo to employees stating that they could vote any way they liked. But he added that they should realize that the company exported most of its products to the United States and if a sovereign Quebec was denied NAFTA membership that would affect their jobs.

"It was not a death threat," he told me in a telephone interview. "Basically it just makes a warning against anti-sovereignty activities. It was vague and it says you stood up against that cause and we let it go last time, but we won't in future. It's a bunch of crackpots and it's not going to stop me."

Two others on the list, Dominion Textile Inc. and Trizec

Corporation, would not comment on the record when called. But Domtex sources told me the letter had been received and the company did not want any adverse publicity so it would not comment. Another source at Trizec said off the record the letter had been received but they wanted to remain low profile. The fourth company I contacted confused me. It was on the list but its owner, Ted Goldman of Canadian Buttons Inc., said he had not received any threatening letters. Just a visit from the provincial referendum watchdog. That was fascinating because it looked like the separatist government might be harassing the companies on Villeneuve's "hit list" at the same time as a person or persons unknown were making violent threats by letter.

There appeared to be some kind of campaign of intimidation, but nothing concrete. I wrote about reports that a St. Hubert storekeeper, not on Villeneuve's hit list, got a letter threatening his life. The letter said he was one of the first group of one thousand "English invaders who will be executed in reprisal for treason committed before the Quebec people last October 31."

His story appeared in the *Suburban* and his identity was protected. But it's frightening that this man said he was never involved in politics. I speculated in a column that this might mean that some people are piggybacking intimidation tactics for personal reasons, because they're nuts, or to drive someone out of their business for some reason.

"I think this newsletter incites hate, should be investigated by police and human rights commissions," I wrote in my *Post* column on March 30, 1996. "Besides that, Canadians deserve to know just how cozy or connected the lawless and the elected in Quebec are. And the sooner the better."

Two days later I got a fax from a Montreal businessman who was on the hit list, but whom I had not called. I telephoned him immediately.

"You are the only journalist with guts to write about this stuff. When I read your column and you wanted to know just how cozy or connected the lawless and the elected were in Quebec I had to tell you my story" said Randy Rotchin, president of A&R Dress Company Inc. in Montreal. He faxed me a copy of a threatening letter in French on the old FLQ letterhead, a copy of his police complaint, and a copy of the judgement against him by referendum authorities. His documentation linked terrorist intimidation, government harassment, and Villeneuve's hateful newsletter. The FLQ might be back in business and that was a story of national importance in Canada. We all remember being riveted to our television sets during the October 1970 crisis. The events were alarming: the kidnapping of British diplomat James Cross; the communiqués by the FLQ; the imposition of martial law and calling in of troops; the incarceration of Quebecers without normal civil rights being adhered to; the kidnapping and murder of Liberal cabinet minister Pierre LaPorte in a seedy motel near Dorval Airport. These were flashpoints in Canadian memories.

But one swallow does not make a summer, so before linking a former FLQ terrorist and his newsletter to a resurrected FLQ I needed another victim or two.

So I faxed all remaining companies on the hit list, requesting information. I wanted to run with a story as soon as possible and gave each one two days to reply. I asked them to send me a copy of whatever threats they had received. The very next morning, I got what I needed. Most of the others never answered.

But Montreal-based Jack Spratt Mfg. Inc., another garment manufacturer, fired off a fax confirming that they got a letter and a visit from a government official. One of the owners sent a copy of the letter, which was identical to the one sent to Randy Rotchin. The letterhead logo was a portrait of a bearded, toque-clad peasant, or habitant, carrying a rifle and smoking a pipe. The *Post* library obtained a copy of the logo used back in the 1970s by Villeneuve and others. Bingo. It was the same habitant, only drawn more primitively. Likewise, the letters ended with a poem about

"La Tempête." That was the name of Villeneuve's newsletter. The poem stated that anyone who stood in the way
would find himself in the midst of a violent tempest. The
separatists were deliberately turning up the heat.

Before writing my story, however, I had to call Villeneuve
and ask him directly whether he and his followers had resurrected the FLQ and were involved in the letter campaign.
I called around and got his private unlisted home phone
number within an hour, from a television journalist. I couldn't
get a tape recorder for the conversation, but used the
speaker phone and asked my executive assistant, Barbara
Maxwell, to witness the conversation. I did this just in case
he made a threat over the telephone. I wanted evidence so
that I could lay criminal charges against him. He denied any
connection to the letters or government harassment.

"I have nothing to do with that [the FLQ letters],"
Villeneuve told me in the interview. "My Mouvement is a
political entity now. There is no FLQ now."

I quoted the letters that claimed to be from a resurrected
cell of the former FLQ: "The 'Front de Libération du
Québec' is reorganizing. We know that you are responsible
for underhandedly trying to influence the vote in favour of
the 'No' side in the last referendum. For us, it is unacceptable that a gang of conmen like you terrorize honest workers through blackmail and psychological terrorism.

"We are giving you a chance this time. At no other time
henceforth will we allow you to act in this manner. We are
warning you that actions will be taken against you and
your business, to mitigate the damage inflicted by the dom-
inant Canadian powers on the Québécois people."

Other companies on the "enemies" list were contacted
but refused to comment. One businessman said he got the
same letter but was "fearful" of the consequences of going
public with the contents.

But Randy Rotchin, who sent me his letter after my initial column about threats, told me he went to police.

"Even more disturbing to me was the supreme indifference

(maybe even negligence) by the RCMP when I contacted them for help. When I called the RCMP and described the threat against me and my company, I was told that this was not a matter for them, and I was advised 'to call 911,'" he said. He called 911 and two local police arrived but were not enthusiastic about pursuing the matter because the letter was untraceable.

It was interesting to me to recall that after the referendum a letter was published by the *Suburban*, allegedly from some anglo assault group threatening violence in the event of separation. The editorial staff treated the letter as a hoax, but the RCMP and Quebec Provincial Police paid an unsolicited visit to editor Christy McCormick immediately after publication of its contents.

"What frightens me the most is the possibility that there is a connection between these terrorists and the government. Otherwise, why is nothing done to find out who sent these letters?" asked Rotchin.

A&R employs 1,100 Quebecers, directly and indirectly, making garments mostly for export to the United States. During the referendum his "crime," which made him an "enemy" of Quebec, was merely to point out in a letter to his workers that if Quebec seceded and was out of NAFTA, they might be out of work.

His letter was cited by Villeneuve's newsletter as evidence that he was one of Quebec's "enemies." His letter to employees also got him in trouble with Quebec's elections officials. They charged him with violating the Referendum Act, which required that any Yes or No message during the referendum campaign had to be approved by official Yes or No Committees, who had partial government funding and spending limits.

"Two months after the referendum, I was visited by an agent of the Chief Electoral Office of Quebec and charged with violating two counts of the Electoral Act," he said.

The same letter about NAFTA and secession he gave to his workers before the referendum was cited as the reason for the "violations."

"I asked the official to give me the name of the complainant but he declined," he said. "I told him my idea of democracy was that I could face my accusers. And the official replied, 'Not in this province.'"

"I feel just helpless. I'm sitting here watching this beautiful city going down the toilet economically due to the uncertainty and pandering to these kinds of people," he said.

I interviewed others. Robert Goyette, president of Charette Transport Ltée. warned his employees in a letter during the referendum about the consequences of a Yes vote and made the hit list. But he did not receive an FLQ letter.

"An officer called and asked to see me. I didn't see any reason to talk to him because I still think that I have the right to express my opinion like any other Canadian," he said in a telephone interview. "I told him if he wanted to see me he could go to court and get the power to get me to answer questions."

Ted Goldman of Canadian Buttons got no letter but said: "Somebody got hold of that list in government. All we said to employees in a memo was make sure you vote the way you want but our company policy is that it's important to stay in NAFTA to keep jobs," said Goldman. "We got a letter from the government saying you contravened the bill because you're not in the budget of the No Committee for the money you spent."

"Then some other idiot came in to tell me he was from the referendum council and he didn't think it could go further with this because they figured we spent $10 to $15 communicating with our workers. It was so foolish it was not worth talking about."

This was a front-page news story, not another opinion piece. To amplify the news, I called CTV, who agreed to run the story that night on their national newscast in return for exclusivity. The *Post* and CTV had enjoyed a special relationship and I had given them scoops the day before the stories appeared in our pages in return for a mention of the newspaper. The CBC was hopeless, with anchors like Peter

Mansbridge who were part of the problem, keeping off their airwaves alternative views regarding Quebec. In one instance during the referendum, the CBC did a two-parter interviewing three allegedly unbiased Quebec voters. One interviewee was Dermod Travis, who was described as an undecided voter but who, during the referendum, worked avidly on behalf of the Yes forces and is close to, if not employed by, the separatists, according to Montreal journalist Peter Sauvé.

"I brought this Dermod business to the attention of the show's producer before the second part of the two-parter ran and they still put Dermod on without any disclaimer as to his activities or affiliations. This was poor television," said Sauvé.

The CBC in Quebec was mostly run by separatists. Even outside Quebec, the national network had been greatly influenced over the years by former Montrealers such as network honcho Mark Starowicz. The boys in the Moby Dick recall that he had been a left-wing student activist who sympathized with a movement to impose French on McGill University.

As usual, the rest of the media ignored the FLQ story, even though it was of national importance. The possibility existed that terrorism was around again trying to drive No voters out of Quebec and trying to destabilize its economy. This had huge negative implications for all Canadians.

Here were Canadians intimidated by their provincial government for being loyal citizens fighting for Canada. After Singh's photograph appeared on the front of Villeneuve's newsletter, a brick was thrown through his window. Then he got telephone death threats.

"There is racism involved here against me and others. The civil service is 99 percent French. The civil service of Montreal is 98 percent French and also has not allowed people of other origins in for twenty-five years," he said, adding that, "Personally, I believe most French-speaking people are not racists.

"I'm not against French Canadians. If they break up the

country they'll lose their heritage and lose half of Quebec, because loyal people like myself will demand that Montreal and the native regions remain in Canada and we will fight and do whatever is necessary to do that."

The cartoonist, Anthony Bonaparte, had also received threats.

"I'm black and an anglophone and I got fed up," explained Bonaparte in a telephone interview. "That's why I drew Parizeau and Bouchard in Klansman's outfits, it was the day after Parizeau resigned for making racist comments."

After his cartoon ran, the French press vilified Bonaparte for being a racist. Only in Quebec would a black man be called a racist for depicting racism. "The anti-fascist league got into the fray and called me a fascist. After the newsletter came out, I got a death threat message left by a French person on my answering machine. Then I got a second one so I called the police. They said there was nothing they could do about it. I worry sometimes, wondering whether someone is going to throw a Molotov cocktail through my window. I plan to move house. I do editorial cartoons and I had to think long and hard about my next cartoon after this happened. It's in the back of my mind. But I feel that I've got to keep on doing what I've always done.

"I'm a bilingual Quebecer who has lived here most of my life but I'll never be a Quebecer in some people's eyes. My immigrant parents chose to put me in French school so I could assimilate. Now I speak French but it's not good enough."

Whether planned or not, what appeared to be happening was a post-referendum strategy of intimidation to drive out "ethnics" and "money." Some separatists were obviously out of control. The province looked the other way and Ottawa turned a blind eye. The heat had to be turned up.

After looking at the law and talking to a lawyer in Montreal, I wrote in my column that I believed Villeneuve's publication constituted a Criminal Code offence under the "hate propaganda" section and should be investigated by police. I also suggested that Parizeau's parting speech might be an offence. After all, individuals and corporations on the newsletter's hit list had been victimized either by threatening letters, phone calls, or government harassment. I then published more excerpts from my interview with Villeneuve.

I asked him if he felt violence was necessary again. If not, I asked him why he named a "hit list" of "enemies" who he said should be pushed out of Quebec.

"No [I don't support violence]. Now there are no conditions for violence. I wrote the newsletter [list] because I like to defend some ideas I have," he said.

I asked him whether he didn't realize that, given the threats that those mentioned in his newsletter received, it constituted inciting hatred?

"I don't think we inspire hate," he said.

Don't you think labelling these people as "enemies" is designed to get people to hate them because people hate enemies? I asked.

"I think there are a lot of English Canadians that are enemies against Quebec people," he answered.

What about your newsletter's suggestion that these people should be driven from the province?

"I don't think I go so far," he replied.

Villeneuve's list of people had demonstrably become victims, in one way or another. This meant they could sue in civil courts for damages. The law was clear on this, as far as I was concerned: "Section 319. (1) [Public incitement of hatred]. Every one who, by communicating statements in any public place, incites hatred against any identifiable group where such incitement is likely to lead to a breach of the peace is guilty of (a) an indictable offence and is liable to imprisonment for a term not exceeding two years."

And Section (2) might apply in Parizeau's case, I suggested: "(2) [Wilful promotion of hatred] Every one who, by communicating statements, other than in private conversation, wilfully promotes hatred against any identifiable group is guilty of (a) an indictable offence and is liable to imprisonment for a term not exceeding two years."

There were defences only if the statements were true, if they were stated in good faith or constituted an opinion on a religious subject, or if the statements were in the public interest and for the public benefit.

None of the defences applied and yet the separatists continued to get away with racist comments and racist attitudes. That was bad enough, but more scandals surfaced the next day in an interview with a spokesman for the Cree nations.

10
The Crees

The same night we were drinking at Moby Dick's in Montreal (March 5, 1996), a blue-ribbon assemblage of various big-shots met in Ottawa. Some one hundred "prominent" Canadians had been invited to attend a think-tank. The goal was to hammer out a deal that could keep the country together. It was sponsored by the Business Council on National Issues and organized by its executive director and Ottawa lobbyist, Tom D'Aquino. It was a two-day event. I decided against going because I felt it was simply a waste of time, with the same old players and same old ideas containing the same old taboos that had brought us to the brink.

Participants included ranking Liberal and Tory appeasers, big-business types, Charlottetown Accord supporters such as Ovide Mercredi, and the usual Quebecers. Brent Tyler jokingly dubbed them "the Meechkins."

Two days before the conference, a Montreal lawyer named Andrew Orkin called me. He identified himself as a lawyer for the Cree Indians in Quebec. He wanted my help.

"We called you because you have been writing terrific

stuff and you understand what's going on here," he said. "We want Chief Matthew Coon-Come invited to the Ottawa conference and they aren't letting him in. I called D'Aquino and he said there just wasn't room for the chief."

He wanted a column written about this snub. He called them "the prominent Canadian Constitutional Tinkerers" and pointed out that Ovide Mercredi had been invited to represent all aboriginals, in spite of the fact that many had opposed Mercredi's endorsement of the Charlottetown Accord. "That's fine, but wouldn't you think this prominent group of Canadians would want to involve the aboriginals who live in Quebec to discuss the future of Quebec?"

That made sense to me.

"It is imperative that the Quebec First Nations partici- pate in this event. It seemed to us that people in Quebec are the real important issue. There will be an information deficit unless First Nations people are there from Quebec. Given the Crees' prominence in holding a courageous ref- erendum in October, it's hard to believe a group of one hundred prominent Canadians would regard themselves as comprehensive if Matthew Coon-Come was not there. We were told by D'Aquino that the list was closed. There are loads of Québécois, but not one representing the original inhabitants of Quebec."

We agreed to meet two days later in Montreal to discuss that and other issues. "You were the first one to write about the Crees and their stand against separation and that's why we wanted to talk with you," he added.

He showed up on a Saturday afternoon at Sir Winston's Pub near Moby Dick's. Tall and red-bearded, he was from South Africa, where he had been active in the fight against apartheid.

His role was very important. He had pulled together the relevant legal cases, and incorporated them in an impres- sive bound book stating the legal right of the aboriginal peoples to opt out of separation. The book had been part of an elaborate and expensive press kit handed out during the referendum to two thousand journalists and law firms in Canada and around the world. The effort had cost the band $500,000. The book made the case, in terms of international law, that there was no way the Cree or Inuit could be removed from the Confederation of Canada by a separatist regime, or even by consent of Ottawa. It was a tour de force which, as usual, got scant attention in the media during the referendum. But like Guy Bertrand, Stephen Scott, and the Equality clan, the Crees argued compellingly that those who wanted to take Quebec out of Canada were conspirators to an illegal act. The difference was the Crees used international legal arguments. They also used emotional ones.

"In 1971, the Quebec government announced that it planned to divert and dam all of the great rivers on our lands," said Cree Chief Coon-Come in a speech in Vancouver several months after the referendum. "It was then we became aware of the significance of what had been going on all of those years when our lands were changing hands between kings, princes, and countries.

"The governments and courts had led us to believe that we were squatters on our own lands. Meanwhile the destruction of our lands and rivers continued daily. This new project to make a country called Quebec is being undertaken on a foundation of double standards. It is being stated that, whether the Crees consent or not, we will be forcibly included in a new independent Quebec. Our treaty with Canada was never intended to permit the international kidnapping of an entire people. If this constitutional arrangement is repudiated by the separatists, they cannot unilaterally claim the benefit of provisions that favour them such as the extension of Quebec to include our lands while at the same time claiming that others do not apply, such as the Crees' treaty and constitutional relationship with Canada.

"We Crees were told by the separatists that if we were to dissent against our inclusion in a future independent Quebec, force would be used against us. We have always deplored violence and declared that we will never use force to achieve political ends. But the government of Quebec has refused to rule out force, saying only that it will use whatever means are necessary, including force, to ensure that Aboriginal peoples' lands are part of a future independent Quebec. What kind of governments are these, that would contemplate the use of force to kidnap an Aboriginal people of 12,000 who have lived where they are for thousands of years?

"We are saying, 'No more.' Matters of self-determination can no longer be decided or imposed. These changes cannot be made without our free and informed consent.

"We are reminding the world that we have the right as a people to determine our own destiny and the right to choose to continue our treaty relationship with Canada."

The chief criticized Chretien's rushed proposals for "distinct society" status and special veto powers for Quebec, initiatives that were cobbled together after the referendum. Among criticisms, he noted how it was foolish to give veto power over changes to a government that has the goal of separating from Canada. He then raised a serious concern about the motivation of the federal Liberals.

"For more than three years before the 1995 referendum we called upon the federal government to declare that if Quebecers have a right to determine their future, then certainly so do the James Bay Crees. We undertook a poll, and discovered that if the federal goverment were to declare that it would defend our right to choose to remain in Canada, up to a quarter of the Yes voters in Quebec would change their minds or become undecided. But for some reason the federal government refused to declare that it would uphold the Crees' treaty rights and the Constitution of Canada."

The Crees' elaborate efforts during the referendum had been torpedoed by dirty tricks, not by separatists, but by someone in Prime Minister Chrétien's own office who, on the same day as the release of their press kit and book, leaked a contrary legal opinion as to their right to remain in

Canada. It was sabotaged by someone in the highest office of the land and the prime ministerial message was seized by the separatists to rebut all the Crees' arguments.

"Someone in Ottawa went so far as to leak an unsigned privy council memo to the press on the same day last September when we released our study on our right to choose to remain in Canada in the event of Quebec secession," said Orkin. "This memo, which could just as well have been written by the separatist government of Quebec, is now part of an information package on the question of Aboriginal rights in Quebec that the Government of Quebec sends around the world. Essentially, this document stated that the best policy would be for the federal government to stand at the border if Quebec secedes, and wave the Crees, and our lands, goodbye."

True to form, the Quebec press gave this unsubstantiated privy council memo the same coverage as was given to the Crees' five-hundred-page legal brief.

The leaked document stated: "The right to remain Canadian could be repudiated by getting assurances from Quebec they'll be well treated."

"The separatists reproduced this by the thousands to counteract our arguments and it succeeded," said Orkin. "Imagine someone inside the Prime Minister's Office itself undermining the country like that?"

I found this shocking because someone in the Prime Minister's Office agreed that Quebec could force the Crees and Inuit to leave Canada and relinquish their citizenship against their will. Here was someone in the federal government saying rights enshrined in the constitution could be repudiated if the separatists promised to treat people properly. In essence, this opinion said Ottawa by fiat could abandon, or pick and choose, citizens.

It was also shocking because the Crees and Inuit represented a more homogeneous group controlling a better-defined territory than francophone separatists did. The First Nations' lands had been given to Quebec in the twentieth century. They were not part of the province when the nation was formed, which meant there was even less justification for denying them the right to choose to return to their previous status as a Canadian territory, not part of Quebec, should separatists pull off secession.

What was going on in Ottawa? Were the Prime Minister's Office and federal government infiltrated by separatists or their sympathizers? Were the Liberals just taking orders from the separatists who ran rampant in the Quebec wing of their party? Was the document doctored? Was anyone attempting to track down who leaked it and why?

The tactic worked. After all, the Crees provided the most sympathetic case for partition and against separatism around. And yet the Canadian federal government was sabotaging their efforts.

"I see little difference in some ways between apartheid there and here, although Quebec is not a sustained reign of terror. It's harassment, intimidation, and illegal discrimination against anglophones and aboriginals," said Orkin.

Over a few beers, he provided more damning information about collusion and indifference on the part of the separatists and federal government.

Despite such manoeuvres, the most effective federalists in Quebec had been the Crees. When the hideous Bill 101 came into force in 1978, the gigantic Sun Life Assurance left town along with thousands of anglos in the financial community. But the Crees rioted against the requirement to send children to French-language schools, and other language restrictions. Traditionally, English had been their second language after their native tongue, and they steadfastly refused to give up its use. Quebec had to send riot police in to force them to use French in government offices, signs, and schools. Resistance continued until the Crees and the Inuit (who occupy the northern third of the province) took their case internationally and appealed for help. The Quebec separatist government backed off and the aboriginals were exempted from Bill 101.

During the referendum the Crees were once again the separatists' toughest opponents. They held their own referendum days before Quebec's. The Inuit did likewise. They also played real hardball by sending out a damaging letter about separation to U.S. buyers of Quebec government and hydro bonds on the eve of the referendum.

Chief Coon-Come sent a ten-page letter to America's biggest investors, underwriters, and securities officials, outlining concerns. In a nutshell, the chief wanted Americans to know that legal title to two-thirds of Quebec (Cree and Inuit lands) did not belong to either Hydro-Quebec or a breakaway provincial government.

Spokesmen in the office of the Quebec finance minister, Bernard Landry, refused to comment on the Cree letter, but faxed me a copy of a December 21 Standard & Poor's analysis of Quebec bonds that rated them A Plus with a stable outlook.

"S&P notes that if the Yes side had won, the rating outlook would have been immediately changed from stable to negative." S&P said that assuming a peaceful transition to sovereignty, an independent Quebec's rating would be in the "single A range."

That was a silly assumption, according to the chief's lengthy letter to investing Americans. "By violating both Canada's constitution and the agreement, the PQ government is putting into grave doubt the future control over hydroelectric and other resources or projects in our territory. Any resulting disputes would have to be resolved peacefully and equitably according to the applicable rules under international and Canadian law. Unfortunately, these rules are far from clear and Quebec's unilateralism would unavoidably lead to protracted litigation and conflict."

He pointed out three further problems that bondholders should understand: 1) There was no "legal precedent" for secession, which means years of court battles. 2) "A secessionist Quebec may ultimately find itself without a significant portion of territory which is currently included. At the same time, the province could find itself responsible for the outstanding debt of the James Bay hydroelectric project that would no longer be within its jurisdiction." And 3) international law did not require the Crees of Canada to assume any portion of the debt incurred by Quebec or Hydro-Quebec in relation to the James Bay hydroelectric project. "Negotiations would have to take place with no certainty as to their outcome."

He also added that he regretted writing this letter because "under normal conditions" Quebec is a good place to invest and its people are generally tolerant.

"However, the present separatist government in Quebec prefers to opt for a strategy that threatens insurgence and instability," he concluded.

The letter was sent to the Securities and Exchange Commission, Moody's International, Dominion Bond Rating Service, and all the governors of the New England states. Those jurisdictions were involved because Quebec supplies New England with about 25 percent of its power and New York with 10 percent. And if, due to wrangling, power distribution were interrupted, virtually all power to that region would be interrupted. That is clearly a grave strategic concern for Washington, which is why the chief also sent copies to the U.S. State Department.

The Crees were astute when it came to garnering support beyond Canada's borders. After all, they had single-handedly defeated further expansion of hydroelectric power in their lands by lobbying American politicians in alliance with American environmentalists.

All this cunning was fuelled by the wealth that the Crees had acquired as a result of the original James Bay hydro agreement, I surmised. I was wrong.

"The Cree negotiated the James Bay agreement after the bulldozers were sent in without their permission," said Orkin. "With a gun to their heads they agreed to a lump sum amount of $225 million in 1976 with no royalties on the power sales afterward. Now, twenty years later, the damages to their economic life are uncompensated for. There has been mercury build-up in the reservoirs created by the hydro project so they have been unable to fish in most lakes. Twenty percent of Canada's boreal sub-arctic forest has been leased to logging companies by the hydro utility. The forests are in their lands and they will all be gone in fifteen years, which means there will be no hunting."

The Crees occupy an area the size of France, in isolated villages. Some $3 billion worth of mineral and forest and power wealth is exported annually out of their territory and they do not receive a dime, added Orkin.

Worse yet, the $225 million is nearly gone and was earmarked for providing infrastructure and services that other citizens don't have to pay for out of their own pockets such as hospitals and schools. The lump sum payment, in other words, was not compensation for property but advance payment for government services.

I mentioned to him statements a few months before the referendum that made me wonder whether the Crees were being tough on separatists to get more money out of Ottawa or, alternatively, out of Parizeau, who had briefly retained the Indian and Northern Affairs portfolio of his goverment. A $30 million grant had just been awarded to them from the federal government, which smacked of extortion.

"The $30 million was a twenty-year-old promise just made good. It was used for emergency sanitation systems. Years before we had an outbreak of serious gastrointestinal infection that killed many. Bill Diamond [one of the tribe's leaders] has a son that is retarded because he had a sustained fever as a result of the epidemic.

"By contrast, the 20,000 Newfoundland fisherman have received $3 billion in economic compensation over the loss in their fishery in just three years," he said.

The Cree chief was not an enthusiastic flag-waver when it came to remaining part of Canada. There is an affection but there are also deep wounds as far as past treatment is concerned. The Cree strategy was also not to play both

against the middle in order to become an independent aboriginal state, as some Liberals told me.

"The Crees know they cannot exist as a nation-state and
have no desire to," he said. "They also do not want to be
enclaved in an impoverished, over-indebted Quebec state.
That is not an option. The Crees are not stupid."

Loyalty towards Canada was keen among the Crees. He
said that the chief's council had many debates about how to
word the question in their own referendum. They knew
that they could guarantee a No outcome if it was made
clear that a Yes vote meant separation from Canada. The
question read:"Do you consent as a people, in the event of
a Yes vote in the Quebec referendum on October 30, to
have Cree lands separated from Canada?"

"The word Canada in all three languages in that question
pushed all the Cree buttons. Crees have no interest being
part of Quebec or being alone," said Orkin.

The referendum was a logistical nightmare. Because the
Crees are scattered throughout an area the size of France,
the leadership had to hire four helicopters to find voters.
The total cost, including the fancy book stating the international law case, was $2 million.

"Here you have a monumentally expensive effort to
save the country mounted by one of the most impoverished
citizen groups in Canada," he said. "They had to get money
for the type of sanitation that all Canadians should expect.
They have a huge housing shortage and are living eleven to
a three-bedroom house on average. They are short one
thousand housing units and on the backs of these poor citizens the referendum battle was fought better than the
Liberals or feds or No Committee fought it."

Some 77 percent of eligible voters cast a ballot with a
resounding 96.3 percent No result. The Inuit had a similar
result in their own referendum. Then Orkin described
another abuse that had not been publicized.

After the Crees announced the No vote in their own referendum, some aboriginal leaders began to get concerned

about the closeness of the Yes-No vote in the province as a whole, according to newspaper polls. So instead of boycotting the separatists' referendum, many decided to vote for a second time in the October 30 referendum.

But on October 30, many found they could not vote. I decided to investigate whether this was true, and began a series of phone calls the next week. Orkin was correct. The separatists had disenfranchised a large number of Crees through more dirty tricks.

"We were not sure we wanted to participate and when we tried to there was some kind of an obstruction," Bill Namagoose, executive director of the Grand Council of the Cree said in a telephone interview. "On referendum night, there were all these people who were told they could not vote because they were not on the voters' list. Regulations [Quebec referendum rules] came out and it said they would take the band list as maintained by the government."

This voters' list has traditionally included the number of Crees who were officially "treaty" or status aboriginals, according to the requirements of the Indian Act. This had been the practice in past elections as well as in the Charlottetown Accord referendum, said Orkin.

"In our case, the Cree beneficiary list is maintained by the Quebec government itself and we understood they'd take people off that list and put them on the electoral list. That didn't happen. They did door-to-door enumeration. People did vote, but there wasn't a great effort made to enlist the Crees even though we were led to believe they would take the band list."

In one town of three thousand residents, a Cree spokesman said, there was only one person, and a non-native to boot, to enumerate every voter door-to-door. "The enumeration officer did not make a great effort," he said. "This was a crime against democracy."

The allegations should be investigated by federal justice authorities or by the United Nations, I wrote.

Constitutional expert and Osgoode Hall Law School professor Peter Hogg agreed in my interview with him. "It sounds to me as though there probably is a breach of the Constitution. If they [Quebec] used methods of enumeration the effect of which was to discriminate against a group such as aboriginal people, and it sounds to me as though there's at least a prima facie case, that would be breach of Section 15 of the Constitution.

"This is the equality guarantee of the Charter of Rights. What Section 15 requires is that governments treat people equally without discrimination, including discrimination by race," he added.

My column ran and no one else in the media picked up the story and ran with it. There was silence among the Liberals in Ottawa too and no indication that justice officials were looking into a flagrant case of voter disenfranchisement by the government of Quebec.

That was bad enough. Then Orkin said he and two others had undertaken a study of the referendum process itself and found out that the entire vote appeared to be a case of widespread voting fraud as pervasive as anything that had gone on in Mexico.

This involved the inordinately high number of spoiled ballots in the referendum, 1.8 percent of ballots compared to 0.6 percent in the Charlottetown Accord referendum run by federal electoral officials. Quebec newspapers had uncovered the fact that in some ridings, anglophone No ridings, separatist election officials had refused to count ballots where the Xs had not been exactly in the designated circle or because the pencil pressure had not been hard enough.

That pressured Quebec's chief electoral officer to investigate. But he only agreed to do so in three ridings, not province-wide. These three were chosen on a basis of rigged criteria.

Suspicious of anything the PQ government did, Orkin approached two polling experts from McGill University to undertake a study. It took them months and they had to fight to get the computerized polling results through Access to information procedures. The task was tedious because they analysed each of Quebec's 22,000 polling stations. The results came out in April and were shocking.

Their conclusion was that "electoral bias, manipulation or fraud involving scores if not hundreds of polling stations" had taken place. The media mostly ignored this.

But Orkin and McGill University statisticians Jaunsz Kaczorowski and Professor Maurice Pinard proved there had been a massive cover-up. In February, Quebec electoral officials had announced the criteria for the recount, ordering the reopening and recounting of only two hundred ballot boxes. The criteria were scandalous. Ballot boxes would only be opened if they were in ridings where the overall rejection rates were 2 percent or more. And only boxes with 10 percent or more spoiled ballots would be recounted.

Theoretically, under the separatist criteria, a few dozen polling stations where every single ballot had been spoiled within a riding that had less than 2 percent overall spoiled ballots would not be subjected to scrutiny. Their study exposed this scam.

"We found nineteen polling stations not being recounted with a rejection rate of 10 percent to 20 percent because the riding overall was less than 2 percent rejection rate," said Orkin. "From a statistical standpoint, 567 polling stations had rejection rates that would be considered extreme and another 258 stations had rejection rates that are questionably high.

"There should be three times more recounts than the two hundred or so they have looked at," said Orkin. "They should also look at the fact that in the Yes areas there were virtually no rejected ballots. Rejections took place in No ridings for political purposes. Up to 58 percent of ballots were rejected in certain polls. We feel that up to 60,000 votes were improperly rejected and that's charitably assuming a 1 percent rejection rate. Charlottetown was a 0.6 percent rejection rate."

This finally explained why the separatists did not ask for a recount, even though they had lost by only 52,000 votes.

Orkin and his colleagues had uncovered what appeared to be a massive conspiracy to defraud the country as well as a massive cover-up of the conspiracy. To put the fraud into perspective, Orkin pointed out that if the separatists had succeeded in spoiling just three more ballots per polling station, they would have stolen the referendum and plunged the country into a crisis.

11
The Belfast Model

Two days after my meeting with the Cree strategist, Bouchard began a series of public relations stunts designed to give several false impressions. The first was his March 12 meeting with four hundred hand-picked anglophones in Montreal. The purpose was to give the impression that he wanted to include, not exclude, anglos from his vision for an independent Quebec. He also needed to address, and arrest, the growing partition movement in the city. The question of partition had rattled him in January after he assumed the premiership, and led to his only gaffe, the crack about Canada "not being a real country" and the backlash that created in English Canada.

Bouchard also faced a growing partition movement in Quebec. A poll showed that 78 percent of anglophones and 41 percent of francophones in the province approved of it. And Bouchard knew that without Montreal, Quebec's engine of economic growth, independence was not viable.

But the event was a farce. Invitations were sent only to hand-picked members of Montreal's "lamb lobby." Fortunately,

Keith Henderson and Brent Tyler were able to stir up a fuss in the local media because they were not invited. Bouchard's office capitulated at the last minute and sent them invitations to attend.

Bouchard spoke for forty-five minutes and received polite applause. He would not take any questions from the audience or the press afterwards.

"I have acquired a better understanding of how linguistic and cultural diversity make our metropolis vibrant and unique," he said. But he made no promises to ease language restrictions, in order to reflect the fact that Montreal was a bilingual city.

Bouchard also took the opportunity to criticize partition as a way to "erect ethnic boundaries." This was a cute attempt to make the anglos look like ethnocentrics. The truth was the separatists were. Then he told the audience that another referendum would be held.

As for his ill-considered slight about Canada not being a real country, Bouchard apologized. "I'm well aware that Canada is a very real country for the people in this room and right across Canada. I wish I'd been more careful in the way I phrased a remark I made in January."

Reaction to his farcical event was swift and predictable.

"If Bouchard really meant what he said, he should consider easing the restrictions of Bill 101," wrote Mark Kotler's partition group the next day. "He should consider declaring the Outaouais, the Montreal Region and the Eastern Township areas as bilingual. We are not asking for the impossible, like making Quebec a fully bilingual province. Only those areas where the numbers are sufficient."

Gary Shapiro, who was with another grassroots anglo organization, the Quebec Committee for Canada, debunked what Bouchard said in a press release the next day. "The majority of Quebecers in two referendums have expressed their democratic desire to remain within Canada, yet the current government will not respect this democratic assertion. It cannot claim to respect the democratic process in any way.

"His denial of the democratic process and promise of another referendum does nothing to alleviate the mood of uncertainty in the province that is responsible for the stagnation of the economy and a flight of jobs and capital, particularly in Montreal. He misses the crucial point: the constant threat of separation makes productive cooperation impossible.

"He continues to misunderstand the fact that Montreal's decline is the direct result of the separatist cause and its refusal to respond to the democratic will of the majority. The committee concludes that no negotiation toward a harmonious, united and productive Quebec can take place.

"The government's stance requires action on the part of the federal government to make it known that a unilateral declaration of independence by the government of Quebec will not be considered and that Canada will sever diplomatic relations with any foreign government that recognizes such a declaration. The feds must tell the public how they will deal with a unilateral declaration of independence and what they will do to protect the lives and properties of loyal Canadian residents of Quebec."

With Bouchard firmly entrenched as premier, it was time to stir up the sedition case against him. Nothing had been happening on that front after Tyler failed to get private charges laid in December. Even after I urged parliamentarians in print and privately to go after Jacob and others for conduct unbecoming a member of Parliament, nothing had happened. The rest of the media ignored it, which meant that Tyler and I looked like "weirdos."

If we were the only ones pursuing this course of action, it would die a natural death. So I had to find another person with credibility to comment in favour of laying charges or, at least, having Parliament investigate and discipline Bloc members. The man who would fill the bill was retired Canadian major-general Lewis MacKenzie. I did not know his opinion about the matter, but I could guess.

"Only in Canada could you get away with something

like that. In some countries, people would be executed or waiting in jail," said MacKenzie in an interview. "In Canada, the attitude is, ignore it, it'll go away. There are more important issues. Instead, the media spend a week analysing whether the prime minister had a right or left-hand grip on some heckler in a crowd.

"I'm absolutely amazed that it [Bouchard's and Jacob's communiqué] died with a whimper rather than a bang. We're talking about the fact that other nations would charge the individual and in some cases execute him. If I was commanding the army when that communiqué came out I wouldn't do anything with it other than get a hard copy, get in a plane, parade myself into the minister's office and say this is well beyond the military's capability to deal with. This is a serious national issue. We're talking about inciting mutiny, for God's sake."

Defence Minister David Collenette should be turning the military upside down to get to the bottom of it. He should be ferreting out traitors in uniform. Then he said: "But we always fight so clean."

Despite his disgust, MacKenzie did not think the communiqué, or pressure, would have generated much support, or that high-ranking officers had been part of any kind of conspiracy to pull off a mass defection.

"I don't know for sure but I'd be disappointed and surprised. But if you go to the more junior ranks, there is more potential. Is it no wonder why all the coups around the world have been executed by colonels? The younger ones are less tied to loyalty and perhaps more emotional. You have to appeal to emotion."

Three days after that column, Reform Party defence critic Jim Hart said in an interview that he was going to table a resolution in Parliament to conduct an investigation into the communiqué and Bloc defence critic Jean-Marc Jacob for urging mass defections.

"We are asking for an investigation by the defence committee and are also going to oppose the reappointment [of

Jacob] as vice-chairman of the defence committee," said Hart.

The issue was first raised by Hart after Tyler tried to lay charges. David Kilgour (then Speaker of the House) tried to hush him up by slipping him a stern note cautioning him against making allegations of Criminal Code violations in Parliament. "Kilgour said I could be held accountable for saying that Jacob was responsible for doing something. That's absolutely ridiculous."

For some strange reason, the Liberals were once more using every trick in the book to avoid going after Bouchard or Bloc members. Finally, in March 1996, Reform brought forward a resolution referring the "seditious" behaviour of Jacob to a parliamentary committee and the item was debated for three days during Question Period. The Liberals agreed to support the probe but gutted the resolution's wording by removing any reference to the word "sedition" or any allegations. This meant that the parliamentary committee was simply going to examine Jacob and the communiqué.

After days of revealing debate during question and answer period, the Liberals finally supported Reform's watered-down resolution and referred the communiqué issue to a committee for investigation.

Bloc parliamentarians scoffed at this during the dramatic debate, saying the communiqué was just a "job offer" or, as Bloc MP Gilles Duceppe asserted, Jacob was guilty only of the "crime of opinion. A shame for Canada."

But Reformer Lee Morrison correctly pointed out: "This is not about the right to have an opinion. If you write a communiqué to members of the armed forces asking them to abandon their oath of allegiance that's not opinion, it's an action. If you deliver that message to Quebec military bases, that is not opinion, it's an action. We're talking about deeds here. Bad deeds."

The Reform defence critic, Jim Hart, told the House of Commons: "According to the Bloc Québécois, high-level negotiations were held, agreements reached and senior members of the Canadian military were signed, sealed and delivered. The Bloc's defence critic [Jacob] confessed: 'There were officers who were already prepared to create the nucleus of a Quebec defence staff. There are people who have confided this to me already. Absolutely, even officers.' The minister expects the Bloc member to come forward and give us proof. Canadians want to know why the minister doesn't exercise due process and force the member to tell Canada what he knows and name names."

Bloc Member Michel Gauthier pooh-poohed the notion that the communiqué was seditious. "Sedition is a concerted revolt against public authority. Clearly, this is an exaggeration."

Another Bloc member claimed the entire matter was concocted by Diane Francis, "guru of the Reform Party."

"There was nothing hidden. Setting up an army was always intended," said the Bloc member. "This is the thinking of the BQ, supported by 50 percent of the population of Quebec, which has a point of view as to the way the defence system would exist if the project of independence is achieved. He did not have a seditious intention. Not intend to overthrow. If someone is attempting to foment a revolt, they would not do so in the clean light of day. That would be tantamount to signing one's own death warrant. It's nonsensical. Everyone knows our project is to make of Quebec a real country. Is he guilty of sedition because he said he'd respect human rights? The judge said it was merely a job offer. The sovereignty project will take place following a negotiation period of one year. Only after that process."

Another added: "To be a sovereigntist is criminal? Then 50 percent of Quebecers should be accused of high treason? Nobody in Quebec would ever accept that sovereigntists should be treated like traitors merely because they committed the crime of being sovereigntist."

Preston Manning told Parliament that he warned the prime minister in June 1994 to outline what was, and was not, going to be acceptable behaviour by separatists. He was ignored and matters nearly got out of hand.

"My fear was that the absence of guidelines to define what constituted acceptable and unacceptable behaviour would lead to this," said Preston Manning in an interview in May 1996. "What constitutes acceptable conduct in the event of an attempted breakup of the country or part of Quebec?"

The Bloc missed the point, he added. This may not be a criminal offence but perhaps it should be. The job of the committee will be to define whether it should be or not.

"The Liberal attitude has been to avoid the real issues, avoid the realities of secession, and that is a mistake. We must clarify what constitutes acceptable behaviour. Was this contrary to the rule of law or contrary to peace, order and good government, two purposes why this house exists. Parliament not only interprets laws but it also makes laws. I'm afraid if we leave vacuums, accidents will happen. Things we haven't even envisioned," said Manning.

Collenette had commissioned an internal report by the military legal counsel to look into the matter. He refused to give Hart an internal report on sedition by the Judge Advocate General, who administers the military justice system and acts as the legal counsel to the minister of national defence.

"We were told to use access to information, which is outrageous," said Hart to me in a telephone interview during the parliamentary debate.

While stonewalling Reformers, a spokesman with Collenette's office willingly gave me the report's conclusion on March 18, 1996: "It isn't sedition. It's close," he said.

Just what were the Liberals really all about, stonewalling and sandbagging people such as Hart, who had the guts to try to bring to justice the enemies of Canada? Why had they watered down the resolution sending the sedition matter to committee? Why did Liberal House Speaker Gilbert Parent call the sedition debate the "most important debate in history," then tell Hart that parliamentary precedent dictated that if Jacob was exonerated by the committee

Hart would have to resign his seat because he asked for the probe. "Can you imagine?" continued Hart in the telephone interview. "Let the separatist off scot-free and make the federalist resign?"

The Liberals were once more playing games. Telling was the statement made by Bloc MP Michel Gauthier. He said he applauded them, saying "the Liberals are more reasonable" for gutting the language severely constraining the probe.

Later, when Hart attempted to remove Jacob as vice-chairman of the defence committee, the Liberals intervened. Liberal Party whip Don Boudria attended the meeting to ensure the Liberals voted to keep Jacob in his position.

On March 14, Boudria actually voted in place of a Liberal on the committee who refused to vote for Jacob. The Liberal left the room in a huff.

Weeks later, when the Jacob inquiry began, the Liberals behaved in a bizarre fashion. They agreed with Bloc members to further restrict the parameters of the probe.

"What the Bloc is trying to do is make it very narrow and they don't want to bring in anything else except the piece of paper [communiqué]. Already Collenette said we should be asking questions about Jacob's statements regarding a group of Quebec officers willing to form a command structure," said Hart. "Here we have a member of Parliament admitting to advising and counselling disloyalty. It's unbelievable."

Hart recommended to the committee that Jacob be found in contempt of Parliament for the communiqué, that new rules of acceptable behaviour be established for the future, and that the armed forces draft policies and regulations to guide its members when faced with a communiqué of this nature in future "that conflicts directly with the oath of allegiance and the Defence Act of Canada."

The Liberals and Bloc members ridiculed Hart's statement. Just what was going on?

Then I received a disturbing communication: a copy of a letter allegedly sent to the prime minister by a student living in France, who claimed that plans were afoot to recruit a mercenary force of about 1,500 before the referendum to help seize munitions and facilities. I called military sources around the world, including the famous soldier of fortune Mike Hoare. The allegations didn't check out. I couriered a request for evidence to the student at the French address and the address was incomplete so the package couldn't be delivered. The student had named several publications where, he alleged, advertisements for mercenaries had appeared. Two publications responded to my request for information and both denied running such advertisements.

The question was, who was playing dirty tricks? Was I being set up by separatists? Was it federalists or separatists playing dirty tricks?

A *Post* reader sent another story that had appeared in an ultra right-wing Washington publication called *The Spotlight*. It alleged that the prime minister quietly asked the U.S. government for up to 25,000 American troops to aid Canadian troops to prevent an immediate and perhaps violent secession if there had been a unilateral declaration of independence following a Yes outcome.

A subsequent article had appeared in *The Spotlight* containing an official denial by Ottawa and Washington officials. But the publication said it stood by its story. In an interview, the journalist who wrote it told me he could not divulge his source but said it was a Canadian government source.

Another worrisome piece of information came my way from a journalistic comrade, Scott Taylor, editor of *Esprit de Corps*. He said he had two sources who heard a high-ranking Canadian officer brag before the referendum that he was guaranteed a prestigious post by the separatists after a Yes vote.

Taylor tried to get the two soldiers on the record. They declined because they said the separatists in the military would ruin their careers.

Another article surfaced, quoting Captain Guylaine Codeme of National Defence Headquarters saying that "no list exists" of the location and weaponry of the country's two hundred or so armouries. Then Guy Bertrand told a Vancouver audience that caches of weapons were squirrelled away by separatists in the province.

Besides military plans, damaging diplomatic initiatives had been undertaken just before the referendum vote. Quebec Finance Minister Bernard Landry had written to all the ambassadors stationed in Canada urging them to immediately recognize an independent Quebec after a Yes vote.

The complicity of France's Jacques Chirac was another issue. After all, Bouchard had spent a good deal of time currying the favour of the French while he served as Mulroney's ambassador to France. And during the referendum campaign, Chirac delivered by coming close to the type of "Vive le Québec libre" nonsense that Charles DeGaulle pulled in the 1960s.

Chirac volunteered to go on CNN's "Larry King Live," aired October 23, 1995. Then he received a planted phone question from a caller in Montreal, which allowed him to get involved in the Quebec debate. Here is what was said. The caller asked: "Mr. President, would the government of France be prepared to recognize a unilateral declaration of independence by Quebec?"

Chirac: "The French government do not want to interfere in Canadian affairs."

King: "That was not the question."

Chirac: "You have . . . That was not the question?"

King: "The question was, will you recognize . . . "

Chirac: "Yes, yes, I'm coming. You have a referendum . . . "

King: "Next week."

Chirac: "Next week. And we'll see. And we'll say what we think just after the referendum. But we don't want to interfere."

King: "Well, if Quebec decides to separate, the question was, will you recognize that new government?"

Chirac: "If the referendum is positive the government will recognize the fact."

King: "So France will recognize Quebec."

Chirac: "That is fact, of course, and..."

King: "You have no recommendation to the people of Quebec as to how they should vote?"

Chirac: "I told you I don't want to interfere in the Quebec affairs."

Chirac and others always maintained that they didn't want to interfere with any remarks, then they would make remarks that would constitute interference.

Another incident occurred in February 1996, after the McGill rally put partition on the national agenda. France's foreign minister, Hervé de Charette, had visited Canada and was quoted as saying that his country would not accept the partitioning of a sovereign Quebec.

It was an outrageous statement for a diplomat to make. It also violated the spirit, if not the letter, of the Helsinki Accord of 1975 signed by thirty-five European countries relating to security matters and sovereignty, as I pointed out in a column. The text of the accord reads:

"Section III. Inviolability of Frontiers. The participating states regard as inviolable all one another's frontiers."

"Section IV. Territorial Integrity of States. They will refrain from any action inconsistent with the purposes and principles of the Charter of the United Nations against the territorial integrity, political independence or the unity of any participating state."

"Section VI. Non-Intervention in Internal Affairs. The participating states will refrain from an intervention, direct or indirect, individual or collective, in the internal or external affairs falling within the domestic jurisdiction of another participating state, regardless of their mutual relations."

Chirac and the minister also skirted the United Nations' "Declaration on Principles of International Law concerning Friendly Relations and Co-operation among States."

France should have been publicly rebuked by the prime

minister and put on notice that such comments were out of line. Canada should have demanded an apology or imposed trade sanctions.

By April, it was obvious that the strategy was to tighten the linguistic screws even more in order to drive out No voters. This was more *étapism*. That month, the Parti Québécois hard-liners proposed even more discriminatory laws against anglos based on a report that argued the French language was not sufficiently protected. The only measure to protect it, short of separation, was further legislative intervention, they reasoned.

Tyler put together a letter to the prime minister that outlined the history of abuse. The 1994 proposals threatened to go even further. Plans were to ban all languages except French on commercial signs. (This law had been softened by the Liberals and now allowed other languages on signs but only if the type size was considerably smaller.) They would also deny children access to English schools unless one of their parents was educated in English in Quebec. Access had been extended to children if only one of their parents had been educated in English in Canada, not just Quebec.

(Of course, immigrant children and francophone children were another matter and had been denied entry to English-language schools since the mid-1970s, unless their parents had been transferred from abroad or had obtained a special exemption from the language "police.")

But far more sweeping was the report's recommendation that restrictions be expanded beyond the secondary-school level to CEGEPs, or community colleges. This was draconian, because immigrants and francophones who realize their children should know English too send their offspring to English-language CEGEPs. If implemented, it would also guarantee the demise of these remaining English institutions.

As Tyler pointed out, bans against English in Quebec were illegal and also contravened several international treaties signed by Canada in order to protect civil rights.

"The related measure of applying restrictions to CEGEPS would not be unconstitutional because the constitution only protects primary and secondary schools. It would, however, be in flagrant violation of the [United Nation's] Recommendation against Discrimination in Education and the International Covenant on the Rights of the Child."

Such changes would also take away rights enjoyed by many francophones who put their kids into an English-language CEGEP so they could become bilingual. "Attending an English CEGEP is their first opportunity to learn or improve their English because they cannot legally attend English primary or secondary schools in Quebec and there is no such thing as a French school with English immersion, as it is illegal under the curriculum. It is also forbidden to teach English until grade four and forbidden to teach it for more than three hours per week."

Controversy about such changes resulted in new Parti Québécois proposals in spring 1996 that did not go nearly so far. For instance, a proposal to ban all languages other than French from commercial signs disappeared.

But the sign ban had already been ruled unconstitutional by the Supreme Court of Canada in 1988. It ruled the ban was an infringement of the right of freedom of expression under Section 2(b) of the Canadian Charter. The law was not struck down because then-premier Robert Bourassa invoked the "notwithstanding" clause and Mulroney did not disallow that invocation.

This was a disgrace, considering that the United Nations Committee on Human Rights had held that while Quebec could require the presence of French on signs, it could not prohibit other languages under Article 19(2) of the International Covenant on Civil and Political Rights. Following this UN decision, Bourassa passed Bill 86, which allowed signs to be in languages other than French provided French dominated the space.

Such silly sign laws were an embarrassment, but the most unjust actions involved children's rights. Tyler felt that preventing access to English language instruction for any child in Quebec transgressed Section 23 of the Canadian Constitution. (That was true but unfortunately Section 59 allows an exception for Quebec to Section 23 until the National Assembly decides otherwise. "Paragraph 23(1)(a) shall come into force in respect of Quebec on a day to be fixed by proclamation issued by the Queen . . . A proclamation shall be issued only where authorized by the legislative assembly or government of Quebec."

The assembly never acceded to its proclamation, a failing that is cited by separatists as the reason why Quebec is entitled to ignore protections of Canadians who are members of minority groups, linguistically speaking. Elsewhere in Canada, Section 23 is in force and states that children of citizens whose first language was English or French are entitled to be educated in the language that was the first language of their parents "where the number of those children so warrants."

This clause was tested in the courts in Alberta, where a group of francophone parents took the province to task for not providing French control of schools. They won their case in 1990. But no thanks to Quebec.

Ironically, the Quebec provincial government had sided with Alberta against its French minority. The separatists did not want a precedent on the law books that forced them to treat their anglophone minority properly. Even so, despite that victory for Quebec's anglophone minority, protection had still not been granted to them. Quebec's legislature said it did not have to do so because Quebec had never signed the Constitution and the Charter of Rights and Freedoms and also did not accede to Section 23.

Ottawa should have ignored that and disallowed the legislation.

The mistreatment of Quebec's anglophone minority also transgressed international law, notably the UNESCO Recommendation against Discrimination manifesto signed by Canada and dozens of other countries. That document defined discrimination as "any distinction, exclusion or limitation or preference, which based on birth [parents' ethnicity] had the purpose or effect of nullifying or impairing equality of treatment in education."

"Both the UNESCO Recommendation and the UN Convention on the Rights of the Child adopted in 1989 provide that children have intrinsic rights as human beings, independent of the situation of their parents," argued Tyler. "It was discriminatory at the most basic level, to attribute to or to remove rights from children based on some factual characteristic of their parents. To do so constituted discrimination on the basis of birth or descent."

The UN agreed with his interpretation and published its findings months before the referendum. Again the media outside Quebec with the exception of me ignored this embarrassment.

Once more, protection was left up to individuals when the federal government should have intervened.

The separatists had used the language laws as a form of "ethnic cleansing." They had succeeded over the years in driving out anglophone Quebecers and shutting down or financially disabling English institutions. The francization of business forced more anglos out by requiring employers to discriminate against them in terms of who was hired, who was promoted, and who laid off.

Evidence began coming to light that Bouchard's deficit-cutting measures were also going to include cunning ways to ethnically cleanse. Andrew Male had analysed the figures and found that since Parizeau took over in 1994, 42 percent of anglophone hospital beds had been chopped for cost-cutting purposes while only 2 percent of francophone beds had been. I faxed these figures to Quebec's health minister and never got a reply.

"We're now starting to see them break down civil society," Male said. "People are going to die as a result of these measures. This is awful. This is what they are doing now. Stories [in the *Gazette*] came out after this that several suicides occurred because people were upset that their English hospital was going to close while they were still in treatment."

Tyler continued his unflagging efforts and in March he convinced the rally's organizing group, the Special Committee on Canadian Unity, to sue the blue-ribbon members of the referendum's No Committee for preventing them from broadcasting to voters the significance of Guy Bertrand's case. Sued were notables such as Daniel Johnson, Jean Charest, and Liberal cabinet ministers such as André Ouellet, Alfonso Gagliano, and the prime minister's Quebec referendum lieutenant, Lucienne Robillard.

Tyler's statement of claim alleged that the No Committee at its inaugural meeting, which included Johnson, Charest, and nineteen others, unanimously turned down the Special Committee's application to tell Quebecers about Bertrand's case and inform them that the plan to unilaterally declare independence was illegal.

By the end of March, Canadians remained in denial. Both Chrétien and Bouchard hit new highs in polling popularity. Bouchard as premier was sounding like Mike Harris or Ralph Klein with his deficit cuts.

Then, in late March, Bouchard tried to pose as a business-like leader by staging an economic summit to which he invited business leaders and others. At the outset, he issued a challenge to Ottawa to help finance a high-speed rail megaproject linking Montreal and Toronto. The multibillion-dollar scheme was the brainchild of an archfoe of separatism, Laurent Beaudoin of Bombardier Inc.

The suggestion was an attempt to embarrass Ottawa if it declined to put up funds or, if it did, to co-opt Beaudoin, who had been notably vocal during the referendum against the separatist cause.

Bouchard also pretended that he wanted business leaders to give him their best advice on how to improve Quebec's flagging economy. Then he ignored it. One business tycoon after another told Bouchard that Quebec's economic problems were political. The province was no longer an investment destination because of separatism and the threat of another referendum.

Bouchard dismissed their remarks, saying that people invested in unstable Northern Ireland, so why wouldn't they invest in a separate Quebec?

His example was well chosen. Montreal's Bombardier Inc. had made the biggest "investment" in Northern Ireland since the trouble began, buying a privatized airplane manufacturer from the government of Margaret Thatcher. Of course, what Bouchard failed to mention was that Bombardier had only "invested" in Northern Ireland because Thatcher's government had handed over the company for nothing. Its debts had been forgiven and generous British contracts were part of the deal.

That encapsulated Lucien Bouchard's vision for Quebec. A backwater economy with huge political problems that would only be invested in by companies who were given massive government subsidies and contracts. The Belfast model.

12
The Political Game

Television journalist Benoit Aubin met me in mid-March 1996. He had just written a book in French that exposed exactly what the separatists had planned to do after a Yes vote. As a former editorial writer for the separatist *Le Devoir*, Aubin was considered a Parti Québécois sympathizer. That was not the case now. He was, like Guy Bertrand, thoroughly disenchanted with the separatists as a result of their behaviour during the referendum.

Aubin was one of Quebec's most respected journalists. When seeking contributors to my Quebec referendum supplement in the *Post*, he had been recommended by author Mordecai Richler. "He's very bright and really understands what's going on," said Richler in the fall of 1995. It turned out he was correct. Like Richler, Aubin willingly agreed to write a piece for the supplement and his contribution received many favourable comments.

Aubin, now a television producer, came into the Ritz dining room grinning. He looked like a gymnast in jeans, energetic, stocky, and strong. His right arm was in a sling.

An elbow cast down to his knuckles made it impossible for him to use his right hand. So he smoked and ate with his left hand. He ate very little and talked a lot.

"I never give interviews," he commented, then gave one.

His book contained the contents of a speech Parizeau had secretly videotaped on the day of the referendum. It was to be aired only in the event of a successful Yes vote. The videotape had been screened by Aubin and six other television executives just before the polls closed on October 30. It had shocked him into realizing what was really going on.

Benoit said he went public with the tape to reveal the fact that Parizeau and Bouchard had lied to Quebecers during the referendum. Yes voters were told they would get a good deal out of Canada. They were not told there would be what amounted to a coup d'état the day after a Yes vote. Yes voters were told that the economic negatives were nonexistent. Meanwhile, they were not told that the separatists were bracing for a full-blown crisis the next day if they had won.

"As the referendum looked like a victory it was too much for them. Landry wrote a letter to [U.S. Foreign Secretary] Warren Christopher urging the Americans to stay quiet. They were expecting a currency crisis and also expecting pandemonium and people pouring into the streets to celebrate. They wanted to send clear messages and appeal to calm that they had a plan, an agenda after a Yes victory. So Parizeau made his Yes victory video," he said.

"Parizeau had a few billion dollars to support the dollar. He expected Canadian society to explode and fall like dominoes, rebounding in a dollar collapse in New York, London, and Tokyo. Parizeau even had an arrangement with the Bank of Canada to prop up the Canadian dollar," he said. "CBC and Newsworld, we were told by the separatists, were prepared to go live for eighteen hours a day if there had been a Yes vote. It was going to be another October Crisis."

The separatists also wanted to control the airwaves after their victory, so they assembled the executives for the secret screening. The logistics involved in getting these people together was daunting. After all, they were rivals who would have liked the tape on an exclusive basis. But second, they were all exhausted from masterminding coverage of the biggest story of their lives.

"There were seven media execs in a room forty-five minutes before the polls closed on referendum night," said Aubin. "It was weird. Parizeau had been taped that afternoon and he was stretching a hand out to English Canada. He made promises to anglos and said their status would not change. He said rights would be enhanced. The dollar supported. He said Quebec would keep its membership in NATO, NORAD, and NAFTA. He promised that the presence of Quebec would be felt in Europe much more, mostly in London.

"Parizeau's idea with the video was to take control over the airwaves. It lasted seventeen minutes and he wanted us to view it to get our pledges that we would be prepared to air it. After it was over, there was a brief silence and somebody said, 'Hello, lobsters,'" he said.

The lobster reference referred to Parizeau's pre-referendum gaffe to diplomats. Now the tape was evidence. The referendum was merely a trap and a Yes outcome meant no turning back and dire economic straits.

"The speech hit me because I realized that if Yes won, we had no idea what we were in for in terms of coverage. That same afternoon a camera crew had spent the day with Parizeau and we agreed to a six-month embargo as to the contents of those interviews. He told us in those interviews that if he lost he'd resign," he said. "He never mentioned the military stuff. They may be fools but they are not idiots. They had a plan."

Parizeau's victory speech was indeed frightening and a translated copy was released in the spring of 1996.

"My friends, Quebec is standing tall," began Parizeau. "The people have just affirmed to the world that it exists. This affirmation, serene and democratic, cannot be erased by anything or anyone. A simple and strong decision was made today: Quebec will become sovereign. And because Quebec is now standing tall, it can first extend its hand to its Canadian neighbour, offering it a new contract, a new partnership, based on the principle of equality between peoples....

"Our first task tomorrow will be to remove our Yes and No stickers so that we can rally behind Quebecers' democratic decision. In this spirit of unity, the government will proceed, as it has indicated, with naming new members of the committee which will oversee negotiations of a partnership with Canada.

"Quebec sovereignty won't be declared right away. It could take up to a year before the National Assembly makes the proclamation. That will give us all the time we need to prepare the transition well: integrating the two public services, defining new economic and social policies with our new tools. Nothing hasty, but done with rigour," promised Parizeau.

"Those awaiting Canadian citizenship can exercise their right to Quebec citizenship once sovereignty is declared. We invite all of them to share with Quebecers the exciting challenge of building a new country here.

"In the meantime, we are still a Canadian province. We'll continue to pay the GST and send our taxes to Ottawa. We are still going to receive all kinds of social-benefit cheques from the federal government. Our federal MPs will still represent us until we declare sovereignty a year from now....

"We will take no action that would hinder the current free circulation of goods, people, capital and services between Quebec and Canada and we don't wish to interfere with the free circulation between the Maritime provinces and Ontario. We have decided to keep the Canadian dollar as our currency. This decision is definitive and irrevocable.

"Everyone also knows that Quebec has the will and capacity to honour all of its financial obligations. Chrétien has a heavy responsibility this evening. During the campaign he told Quebecers, on October 18, that the referendum, and I quote, 'is the definitive and irrevocable choice of a country.' In his speech to the nation last week he indicated that it was a 'definitive decision with no appeal.'

"We agree. We can therefore turn the page, respect the democratic verdict and move to a new dialogue which must now begin between Canada and Quebec in the interests of all our citizens and of stability."

After the screening, Aubin went back to his studio and watched the events unfold with a much different perspective. He arrived home at 3:00 a.m. and could not sleep. He feverishly scribbled down notes about the day's events. It was an epiphany of sorts for him.

"I thought these were decent, legitimate folks with a different opinion than I had," he said. "I discovered that the 'problem' with Canada, and Quebec's place in it, was that the 'problem' was not for real. That we lived in a city, Montreal, where people from all different backgrounds shared an urban place and got along just fine. I've lived here for twenty years and have never known of even a fist fight triggered over race. I realized that nationalism was the problem.

"The FLQ, for instance, never had support or legitimacy among francophones. The problem here is not real. It is only political. That referendum confirmed my views. I've become totally alienated from the separatists. I hated this referendum because it illustrated to me that these people are out in left field," he said.

"The political society of pollsters and editors created this campaign and forced it upon our attention. We were totally manipulated by this referendum. Seventy percent of people were not even interested in it, according to a poll we commissioned at the beginning of the campaign," he said.

"This was not about ordinary folk but about two kinds of people fighting for domination of our tax dollars. I had to come a long way. I was, like all Quebec, convinced government was the solution, not the problem. That was wrong."

Parizeau's return to the separatist movement was an act of "craziness" because the 1980 referendum had determined that Quebecers were uninterested in leaving Canada. "But Mulroney and Bourassa controlled the agenda promising solutions to a problem that did not exist.

"The Quebec situation is contagious. Everything that Quebec wanted and was denied was done in English Canada: bilingualism. There was uproar over that in English Canada. Then what happened was Quebec proclaimed itself unilingual. English Canada is a united, monolithic society and francophones are not united," he said.

"Now we have a situation in Quebec where the separatists have created economic hardship for francophones. The only people not losing money on my house are the people at the bank which holds my mortgage. It's pathetic," he said.

The federalists ran a terrible No campaign, because there has never been any incentive for a politician from Quebec to solve the problem. They kept getting elected from English Canada as prime ministers in order to fix a problem that has been make-believe, he added.

"I went back to *Le Devoir* three years after Meech Lake died and asked their political writers, who wrote so passionately about what an insult the loss of Meech was, what the five conditions of Meech Lake were, and nobody could remember. They talked about riots and the need to secede at the time of Meech's demise and three years later nobody could remember what we'd supposedly lost," he said. "The irony is that Montreal is the only Canadian city as Canada describes itself, bilingual and tolerant."

He, like so many francophones, was disillusioned with the separatists and the games that Ottawa and its Quebec prime ministers had been playing. He was losing his living standards and his city was dying and he knew it. Like Guy Bertrand, he could see that to win this game was to lose.

After interviewing Aubin, I took a cab to the Equality Party headquarters several miles away on Sherbrooke Street. The tiny office has been supported financially by two Montreal businessmen, Allan Singer and Bill Sullivan.

Singer had personally challenged the sign bylaw banning English, taking it successfully to the Supreme Court of Canada. Sullivan, a bombastic businessman with an encyclopedic memory of political and legal events, had been politically active for years. A consultant in the computer field, he tried living in Toronto for a year but returned to fight it out in Montreal.

Thanks to Singer and Sullivan's generosity, Equality occupied a narrow space in a half-empty strip mall. Beside it was a boarded-up cinema, another fitting symbol of the strangulation of anglophone Montreal.

Andrew Male organized a day of research and interviews. People came in and out all day long, even meeting with us while we ate lunch at a nearby Abyssinian restaurant. Party volunteers manned the phones and stuffed envelopes as we sat poring over boxes of documents, faxes, and clippings.

Despite my dislike for the separatists, I still retained the belief that English Canada had mistreated French Canadians. But this was mostly propaganda promoted by books like Pierre Vallières's *Nègres Blancs d'Amérique (White Niggers of America)*, published in 1968. It was written just as the U.S. civil rights movement was hitting its stride and two years before the October Crisis of 1970, when Front de Libération du Québec (FLQ) terrorists kidnapped and murdered. Vallières helped found the FLQ.

The book was aptly described by John Robert Colombo in his guide to Canadian literature and history: "Written in the Manhattan House of Detention while the author was awaiting deportation for demonstrating on behalf of the FLQ in front of the United Nations, it is a memoir of disenchantment with Quebec in the 1960s and a Marxist argument for Quebec independence. Vallières likens the condition of the Québécois in Canada to that of the blacks in the United States."

The entire thesis was copycat radicalism and revisionism. Grievances here were hardly equivalent to the abuse, torture, and disenfranchisement of blacks south of the border. Besides that, past misdeeds were not one-sided, nor were the only exploiters rich anglophones or so-called "Westmount Rhodesians." As Neil Cameron had pointed out, the province's poor Irish, Jewish, and other anglophone workers had been equally exploited at the turn of the century. In the countryside, francophones were ruled by a near-feudal system. The king of France centuries before had granted huge tracts of lands to favourites who functioned as lords of the manor.

Former prime minister Pierre Elliott Trudeau put the revisionists in their place in a *Maclean's* interview in 1992: "So it goes that, with myths and delusions, the Quebec nationalist elites falsify history to prove that all Quebec's political failures are someone else's fault: the Conquest, the obscurantism of Duplessis's time, slowness to enter the modern age, illiteracy, and all the rest. It is never our leaders' fault; it has to be blamed on some ominous plot against us."

Trudeau was correct and many myths have been bandied about by the separatists.

"The White Niggers of America was complete myth," said Andrew Male. "French Canadians have been running this place all along. Anglos hired francophones and the reverse wasn't true. A lot of the tension between French and English was country versus city and Montreal versus Quebec City."

But something else was involved, something that had been going on behind the scenes in Quebec. It had to do with a secret organization whose roots were racist and fascist. It was simply called La Patente, or "the thingamajig," and its members have left a legacy that has greatly harmed Canada.

13
La Patente

The Parti Québécois's predecessor was a secret organization, founded in 1926, called the Ordre de Jacques Cartier. Its nickname was La Patente, "the thingamajig" or "the gimmick." The Order had been organized by the French clergy of the Roman Catholic Church. Women were not allowed as members, nor were they ever told of its existence. Husbands would simply say they were going out to "la patente" at the parish.

The organization was anti-Semitic, anti-English, anti-Protestant, anti-foreigners, and anti-anglo and restricted to Catholics. The impact of this clandestine Catholic society still resonates. For instance, La Patente's flag, red bars and a maple leaf, eventually replaced Canada's traditional red ensign flag. And its membership reads like a *Who's Who* of Quebec politics, civil service, journalism, and clergy.

It was officially disbanded in 1965. But its beliefs continue today. Some of its members were responsible in the past for harbouring war criminals from France's Vichy regime and for bringing about the conscription crisis in Quebec, due to their sympathy for the populism of Mussolini and Franco. Out of this shabby past sprang the Parti Québécois. After all, it was La Patente members Marcel Chaput and Raymond Barbeau who vigorously promoted the notion of separation. Chaput, a federal civil servant, was kicked out of La Patente because he went public with its goal of separation. Not surprisingly, Jacques Parizeau and Bernard Landry were reportedly members. So was Dr. Camille Laurin, who authored the detestable Bill 101, which abused anglophone civil rights. Other notables included Trudeau sidekick Jean Marchand, former Montreal mayor Jean Drapeau, and Cardinal Paul-Emile Léger.

One francophone journalist in 1941 described La Patente as a "Ku Klux Klan of French Canada," an anti-Semitic, pro-Vichy "union of cretins and fanatics" plotting a political putsch in Canada. The late senator T.D. Bouchard warned in a speech in 1944 that the order planned to separate Quebec and form a French-speaking dictatorship.

In that same speech, Bouchard also debunked the La Patente mythology that anglos had been oppressors. "I learned that Canadians of English descent were not all cloven-footed and did not all bear horns ... Why had I been led to believe those sillinesses? ... Since my infancy I had been taught that everything the French Canadian had to suffer came from the fact that he was of French and Catholic descent."

Quebec Catholic textbooks even back then were "fictions" designed to glorify the Catholic Church and pillory the English, said Bouchard.

He warned back then that the Catholic-propagated myths threatened Canada as a nation. And he's still correct.

"We must stop a subversive propaganda, intensified by the state of war which has existed for over four years, which could bring us before long to mob rule and even civil war, prompted by a racial hatred insidiously instilled into the souls of French Canadians by a wrong teaching of Canadian history ... The worms are gnawing the roots of the tree of our liberties. Our secessionists, self-made historians with inventive minds, have called to their aid all the forces that appeal most to the popular masses: religion, race, and greed. The new state would be Catholic, French, and corporatist."

And that is exactly what Parizeau and his separatists have carved out of Canada: an ethnocentric, biased, xenophobic, and corporatist new state, which ignores the constitution and some of the rights of minorities. But as of old, the French in Quebec are only surpassed by their Ottawa civil service and political comrades. And English Canada has been played like a fiddle.

Bouchard went on to cite La Patente as a "sinister plot" that "exploited economic bigotry and woolly-mindedness, anti-Semitism, ignorance, and the priest-ridden prejudices of a backward movement tending to bring us back to the social and economic status of the Middle Ages."

He said the election of the Union Nationale and Maurice Duplessis was owing to La Patente. It was the "poorest and most abusive government we have had in the history of our province."

He quoted from a La Patente tract calling for a "revolution that shall be ours, for the true interests of the French-Canadian people. And this revolution that we want shall be practical, efficient, calm and good because it calls for pure, fundamentally Catholic and French men. It is the revolution of the liberated Spain, of the organized Portugal, of France under Pétain."

Their activities were the subject of an exposé about La Patente in a doctoral thesis in 1982 written by Laval University professor Raymond Laliberté. He said the organization had been replaced by the Ordre de Jean-Talon for two years before migrating into the Parti Québécois and other nationalist movements.

A former head of the Quebec teachers' union and leader of the Quebec wing of the New Democratic Party, Laliberté put years of research into his six-hundred-page study. He was not impressed with what he found. "There are a lot of people today who are proud of what the Ordre de Jacques-Cartier

[La Patente] stood for but personally it gives me a pain in the gut," he told the *Toronto Star*'s Bob Mackenzie in an interview in 1982. "We have a government in power in Quebec today [the Parti Québécois] which to a great extent has inherited the ideology and the way of seeing things of the Ordre de Jacques-Cartier."

Laliberté said the order was founded in secret on October 22, 1926, by a group of seventeen French-speaking Catholics in Vanier, Quebec, mostly federal civil servants. Its original aim was to promote French-Canadian Catholics across the country, particularly in the federal civil service. The order led the opposition to conscription during the Second World War, generating enough of a campaign to bring about a referendum on conscription that excluded Quebecers from the draft. Laliberté described this as the order's greatest triumph: The massive No vote by French Quebec in the conscription plebiscite of 1942.

Laliberté said the carefully chosen roster of members reached 11,000 at its peak, with 75 percent from Quebec. They were organized into 450 small cells and were close to the Catholic Church leadership. The oath of allegiance said: "I will obey the orders transmitted to me and will observe the secret imposed. May my right hand always remain ignorant of the good accomplished by my left hand."

There were rituals, a special handshake, and code names. The order infiltrated the civil services but also political offices, from cabinet ministers to school board trustees and municipal councillors and mayors. Union leaders and journalists belonged, including former writer and cabinet minister Pierre Laporte, who was murdered by the FLQ during the 1970 October Crisis. Besides Parizeau and Landry, other political players who belonged were Mulroney pal Roch LaSalle and Péquistes Jacques-Yvan Morin, Denis Lazure, and Pierre Marois. When stories in the *Gazette*, *Toronto Star*, and Canadian Press quoted Laliberté, naming names, several of the alleged members, such as Morin, denied they had ever been members. Others distanced themselves, saying that they had quit long ago. Interestingly, Laliberté said that René Lévesque refused to join the order, as did Pierre Trudeau.

Former Mulroney operative and journalist Michel Gratton, in his 1992 book *French Canadians,* devoted an entire chapter to La Patente. His father had been a member and the order had been founded in his mother's church, St-Charles, in Vanier, Quebec.

"The name La Patente means 'The Thing' or 'The Gimmick' and a former member told me that the name came from the fact that, when asked by their wives where they were spending their evening, men would answer evasively that they were going to their 'Patente.' For some other reason, the members were also known as 'Pieds Noirs' (or Black Feet)— the only logical explanation for that name being the fact that the Order was largely ruled by the church and priests customarily wore heavy-soled black shoes," wrote Gratton.

According to Gratton, La Patente grew rapidly out of the Catholic parishes to fight the Orange Order, or Protestants, and the Irish Catholics, whom they suspected of being the "enemy within." The Irish were to be feared for taking over the Catholic Church and turning it into an English-language institution. La Patente members were also upset about the lack of French schooling outside Quebec, and about discrimination here and there in the workplace and civil service.

In 1966, Gratton's father attempted to recruit him. "I asked him what on earth this secret resistance organization had ever done. He replied that, among other things, the Order was largely responsible for the adoption of the new Canadian flag," he said. "La Patente for years had its own verson of what it thought should replace the despised Red Ensign. I had seen it flying over a gas station on Montreal Road, a red and white flag split by a diagonal line with a green maple leaf in the middle."

Even more prescient, Gratton's father told him that the group had pushed for official bilingualism across the country, something that came into being with Trudeau just a few years later.

The tactics were called "noyautage" or "infiltration and control," said Gratton. They recruited influential French Canadians to take over the governance of organizations, from city councils to the Caisse Populaires, the parish-founded credit unions. There was rumoured influence peddling, or loans given to otherwise unacceptable La Patente brethren by La Patente bankers and Caisse managers.

Its members spurned the Knights of Columbus because they considered it an English organization, wrote Gratton. La Patente also engaged in dirty tricks and other manoeuvres. They liked to recruit real estate developers to ensure that if a French-Canadian family moved out of a French area, it would be replaced by another French-Canadian family. It was a form of French apartheid.

The oath was revealing. "They put a blindfold over your eyes and people would speak in undertones about the greatness of the race ... In its own way, I guess it was pretty tacky too, but it was impressive at the time," former member and long-time federal bureaucrat Jean Caron told Gratton.

The secret handshake was made by pressing the index finger onto the wrist. The password was the acronym VADMA (which, translated into English, means, "You have a double mission, Antoniutti." The double mission was to preserve the religion and the French language. Antoniutti had been the Pope's ambassador to Canada and he had supported French Catholicism, wrote Gratton. This meant there was a direct link to the Vatican. The church financially supported *La Pointe*, a French-language daily in Hull, Quebec, which has supported separatist causes over the years.

The organization disbanded in 1965 after two exposés in newspapers and a rift between factions. One group wanted to promote French within Canada and the other was separatist, explained Gratton. In addition, policies of Premier Jean Lesage, from the takeover of Hydro Quebec to forming the Caisse de Dépôt et Placements du Quebec and other crown agencies, were supplanting the need for their lobbying efforts. Tellingly, Parizeau was a principal adviser to Lesage and Lévesque, the energy minister who took over Hydro Quebec.

"Members were against anything foreign. It backed Premier Maurice Duplessis's 'Padlock Law' banning Jehovah's Witnesses from the province," wrote Gratton. "Quoting La Patente documents, Laliberté writes that they denounced 'the international semitism' ... those businessmen, but also professionals and industrialists, who, to better con the French population, change their Hebrew names to English or French. They defined the Jehovah's Witnesses as anarchists who play into the hands of the Orangemen or the communists."

While these quotes were from 1930s and 1940s documents, the odour of anti-Semitism, xenophobia, and anti-capitalism remained. After all, this was exactly what Jacques Parizeau revealed on the night of the referendum. He said the francophone people had been defeated by "eth-nics" and "money." La Patente was alive and well and living among separatists.

14
The Separatist Conspiracy

It all began to make sense. Separatists were French bigots, clones of La Patente members. They were ruthless, undemocratic, and dangerous. That's why it was important to spend several hours with Guy Bertrand. He had been a Parti Québécois member until 1994 and part of its inner circle. In April 1996, I interviewed Bertrand again for several hours about the Parti Québécois and what Canada could do to prevent them destroying the country.

"We are talking about two hundred people in Quebec who control the whole province. This is a conspiracy and it's been devastating for the people of Quebec. This elite includes professors, union leaders, the press, some actors, some writers, politicians. These two hundred control everyone else just like the mafia. The federal side is nothing in comparison. I never saw an organization so well prepared as during the 1995 referendum," said Bertrand.

"I call it a revolution in sneakers. It's real and prepared and uses propaganda and controls the press. The majority of this inner circle are left-wingers who don't like business men, corporations. They intended to pull off a constitutional coup d'état. As for the military communiqué and other indications of tampering, it is obviously sedition. And they should go to jail. They have no loyalty to this country and the feds have done nothing for twenty years while we [the separatists] attacked, boycotted the flag, booed the national anthem.

"They control the media in Quebec. They can press a button and get an article against something or someone. The day I started my case, the newspapers had big pieces by constitutional experts and university professors saying I was totally wrong. Full page articles. They never wrote or interviewed me for my position.

"When my judgement came down it protected the rights and fundamental freedoms of people and the federal government said 'no comment.' No Quebec journalist went to Chrétien to get him on the record as to why he wasn't supporting my case. This is because the press in Quebec are accomplices to the silence of the No side, which makes the Yes side very, very happy.

"This has been a conspiracy and there should be a public inquiry into the referendum and other matters. The majority of Quebecers did not want separation. The majority was told nothing about the economic consequences for years and those who did were censored or scandalized," he said.

"It's a conspiracy by the two hundred. We never see people in the streets shouting 'Independence for Quebec.' The two hundred control the whole situation with the press and telling lies and committing fraud. During the referendum, Bouchard and Parizeau were blaming English Canada for not recognizing [Quebec as a] 'distinct society.' Every kid believed English Canada was responsible. But the PQ was against 'distinct society' in 1989, we fought against it and the PQ voted against it.

"Then when Elijah Harper, the aboriginal in Manitoba, defeated Meech Lake and 'distinct society' we [the PQ] had a big party with champagne. We had won and everyone was thrilled because 'distinct society' had been defeated.

Then in 1995, Bouchard and Parizeau lie and say English Canada defeated 'distinct society' and Quebecers should quit Canada for that. The Bloc also voted against 'distinct society,' as did Chrétien.

"To confuse you even more, it was the Parti Québécois which first brought the idea of 'distinct society' to the National Assembly in 1981. The recommendation it made at that time was that this clause be added to the Trudeau constitution," he added.

Bertrand said he left the separatist fold in 1994 for a number of reasons. First, he realized that independence would be economically disastrous. If the referendum had been won by the separatists, it would have been based on answers to a "fraudulent" and misleading question. It would have caused a catastrophe, he said.

"It would have led to a unilateral declaration of independence which, considering my court case, would have been unconstitutional. So we just missed a revolution by a few votes. Now if the people of Quebec want a revolution, there is a price to pay for that and the leaders should say it's a revolution and let people decide whether they will pay that price or not," he said. "The PQ wouldn't confess the price."

The price would be bloodshed, first involving the aboriginals, he speculated.

"Quebec needed the army at Oka for a few hundred people. If the Crees decide to remain in Canada how are we going to stop them? If Montreal and its outskirts and the Eastern Townships, 2.5 million people, decide to remain Canadians, how are they going to be controlled and stopped from remaining Canadians? The point is that because Quebec is not homogeneous it cannot be independent."

He feels the support for outright independence among francophones is only 15 percent. The problem is that now after twenty years of propagandizing and inept federal responses, Bertrand estimated that 90 percent of young Quebec francophones are separatist. "The separatists have a joke that every day when they look at the obituaries in the newspapers they see federalists dying and every day in the birth announcements, separatists are born. This is because they have rewritten the history books in schools and never mention Canada, only Quebec this and Quebec that."

Separatist "brainwashing" and "propaganda" is part of the Quebec education curriculum, said Quebec educator Monique Nemni, now managing editor of the Montreal magazine *Cité Libre*. At the McGill rally in January 1996, she gave several examples of educational malpractice. "In one ministry-approved history textbook there is a cartoon to illustrate the British North America Act. There is a beaver labelled Lower Canada pulling a cart and riding on the cart is another beaver labelled Upper Canada. That beaver is holding a flag that says 'superior race,' " she said.

"This is in a textbook currently being used in Quebec. The message being pounded into their heads is that Canada is not their country, Quebec is, and Canada is an oppressor of some sort," she said. "Such references are throughout the Quebec school curriculum, so it is little wonder that many Quebec students say they are not Canadians, they are Quebecers."

Bertrand confirmed that this is part of an organized revisionist movement within the Parti Québécois to advance their cause by pounding certain attitudes into the heads of the youth. He feels that the only reason the separatists lost the referendum after a generation of such propagandizing was because of the "reputation of Canada." "Canada was saved because it was Canada. It was saved in spite of the incompetence of the federal government and Quebec federalist politicians," he said.

Like Benoit Aubin, he had become thoroughly disgusted with the separatists and with Ottawa, which did nothing to destroy them.

"None of this does anything for Quebec. Unemployment is horrible and would hit one million after separation. The separatists are just trying to destroy the country to take away their own piece of it and the feds have no strategy that works.

When I was a separatist we loved the fact that the feds did nothing when we attacked English or the anglophones."

Bertrand has little use for Bouchard, whom he feels did not leave the Tory fold because of the courage of his convictions. "He left because he knew the Tories would be defeated in the next election. These guys, Masse, Bouchard, Bourassa, all have jobs, good jobs. But they do nothing for Quebec. Unemployment is enormous while they try to destroy the country. They never say anything nice about one of the best countries in the world. In a poll in 1996, 83 percent of Quebecers said they would choose Canada as a country to live in. All this referendum business is madness."

After the referendum, Bertrand started his own organization, Citizens for a Democratic Nation. It raises funds to help him further his constitutional challenge against unilateral declaration of independence. He supports partition, but only if there is a successful Yes vote.

"Secession is a catastrophe and partition would be the disaster after the catastrophe. But it is inevitable," he said. "The strategy of Bouchard and the party is to have two referendums. First, a provincial election that will give him the mandate to negotiate, and reject, a new deal within Canada. This will allow them to refuse anything Canada offers and portray it as rejection. Then they hold another referendum on separation in a poisoned atmosphere of rejection. What can English Canada offer Bouchard? Nothing. Everything will be ridiculed. This would create a new momentum. After Meech Lake's demise 70 percent would have voted for independence."

The only hope is that all the anglophones will vote for the Equality Party and elect some opposition in the National Assembly, he said. "The Quebec Liberals are separatists and Chrétien should disavow himself of the entire party and field new candidates."

The feds should also be pro-active and take Preston Manning's advice. Clear-cut rules should be laid down before the next referendum.

"The feds must say that the only question they will recognize is one that directly asks Quebecers if they wish to leave Canada and only if 60 percent agree will that be considered. In addition, 50 percent of a given region must agree to leave too. This double majority must exist. If it does not, that portion of Quebec will always remain part of Canada. It must also say minority rights are non-negotiable for the portions that may negotiate to leave; anglo rights are not negotiable; native rights are not; a land bridge to the Maritimes is not negotiable; and the repayment of interest and principal on the debt on a per capita basis is not on the table," he said.

If the separatists put forward another trick question, then federalists in Quebec should boycott the referendum and the rest of Canada ignore its outcome. "Do not play that game and no country in the world will recognize such a vote," he said.

"The best thing that ever happened in Canada was the Charter of Rights and Freedoms. In 1981, I said to René Lévesque that as soon as the Charter becomes law it will be impossible to become independent without the consent of the other provinces. I suggested we challenge it in the Supreme Court to stop it from becoming law. Lévesque said don't do that. It is not democratic. Instead, we did not sign the constitution and Charter in 1981."

This confirmed another Big Lie told by separatists, which is that the "night of the long knives" in 1981 was a treacherous act of broken promises by Trudeau. The separatists have always used this excuse as the reason why they did not sign the constitution. But Bertrand said the reason it wasn't signed was to make mischief, and also to exempt the province from the constitution and its Charter protections.

For such outspokenness, Guy Bertrand has paid a huge price. Death threats are a daily occurrence, his friends and relatives shun him, and he has been routinely pilloried in Quebec's press. A whispering campaign has begun, with unknown persons alleging that he is just getting even with his old rival Parizeau or that he is a CIA operative or is causing trouble in order to become a federal court judge.

He has lost clients as well as friends. As a litigator in a small province riddled with separatists or collaborators, his stance is definitely a career-threatening move.

"I had an incident with a friend of mine, a judge, who refused to look at me. He said I was the biggest traitor ever and I should have the treatment that countries give to traitors, the death penalty," he said. "I was so shocked I thought about calling the police because it was a threat to my life."

An open-line radio show host in Quebec City, André Arthur, exposed another threat by a judge, made in early 1996 at a social event in Quebec City.

"A superior court judge said the only thing to shut down Guy was a bullet in his head. The judge was named and requested a copy of the taped radio show where André related the story. But he did not sue," said Bertrand. "Of course, they knew I was his lawyer and that he has no fear and no friends either. Just his dog and his wife. He's a very special, courageous man."

Bertrand believed that the political solution would not be found in time, and that the Liberals were to blame. He believed that people across the country had to get involved and the courts had to rule against any attempts to separate.

Canada's political elite had to be circumvented and ignored. The handful of bigots who were running the separatist movement had to be challenged and their bluff called.

He agreed with Brent Tyler, who said, "Where is the rule of law in Quebec for us? It's a fraud. One million lost their civil rights and over 300,000 have left since 1976. The referendum was a scam, so are figures by Statistics Canada as to the number of French speakers outside Quebec. Look at the Ordre de Jacques Cartier and its conduct during the war regarding conscription. And Trudeau was part of that gang."

Finally, in mid-May, after months of pressure and favourable publicity about Bertrand by myself and William

Johnson, the federal Liberals were shamed into agreeing to intervene in Bertrand's court case.

True to form, Bouchard reacted angily, threatening to call a snap election and referendum. An emergency cabinet meeting was held, and on May 14 Bouchard backed off his bellicose behaviour.

"It's the first time in thirty years I saw these guys have their bluff called and they backed off," commented Andrew Male.

Ottawa was finally starting to do the right thing.

Conclusion

Quebec separatism is not a legitimate struggle for self-determination. It is a racially motivated conspiracy that has run roughshod over human rights, fair play, the Quebec economy, and democracy. The separatists should be treated like the ruthless elite that they are.

Because of superior intellect and single-mindedness, the separatists have controlled Quebec's French-language media and the country's political agenda, and by so doing have been allowed to run virtually rampant, by successive Quebec-born prime ministers, for more than three decades.

A failure to understand the enemy and its tactics has been at the root of the Quebec separatist problem. So has political expediency on the part of the three Quebec prime ministers, who allowed the separatists to flout Canada's constitution.

English Canadians still remain in the dark and do not fully understand the extent of separatist wrongdoing. The separatists have cheated. Lied. Hidden facts. Revised history. Disenfranchised thousands of voters. Fraudulently spoiled ballots, then covered up their crimes. They have tampered with the armed forces of the nation. Stripped anglophones and allophones of their civil rights for more than three decades. Purposely driven anglophones out of Quebec. Passed laws that legalized employment discrimination and educational discrimination. Ruined Montreal's economy. Engaged in acts that transgress international treaties Canada has signed, and otherwise embarrassed Canada internationally. All of this has cost each and every Canadian dearly as a result of higher interest rates on mortgages, consumer loans, and government borrowings.

Once again in June 1996, Bouchard was off to New York trying to convince Americans to invest in Quebec. But he only served to drive more away by arguing that separation was inevitable. He said the future Republic of Quebec would remain open for business, will protect minority rights, and he even added that with Montreal's economy in the doldrums, now was the time for bargain-seekers.

Post columnist Marie Josée Drouin is a fellow of the Hudson Institute Inc. and is married to Henry Kravis, one of America's wealthiest individuals. She wrote on June 5, 1996, that Bouchard wouldn't fool the smart money. "Bouchard has invited American business people to take advantage of the next two- to three-year pause to increase their investments in Quebec. With their help he could stabilize Quebec's economy, assuage Montreal's woes and strengthen the case of separation. Oddly enough, American business people are not queuing up to oblige."

As for Bouchard's claims that Quebec upholds minority rights, she pointed out that "the Quebec government announced that student loans to undergraduates studying outside Quebec would be granted only to those attending French universities."

Clearly, the separatists continued to get away with murder, as had been the case for decades. And where have our federal governments been?

Federal justice officials should have disallowed Bill 22 in

1974, Bill 101 in 1977, and all the subsequent acts of discrimination passed by Quebec's Liberal and Parti Québécois regimes. More recently, justice department lawyers should have assisted Stephen Scott and Guy Bertrand with their law cases back in 1995 to fight the separatists' planned unilateral declaration of independence before it gained any currency.

After the referendum, Ottawa justice officials should have investigated whether to lay sedition charges against Bloc Québécois members for sending the communiqué to the military. They should have investigated whether to lay hate propaganda charges against Parizeau for his racist speech the night of the referendum. Defence department officials should have been turning the military upside down to shake out the separatists and determine if there was some conspiracy to take over part of the army after a Yes vote.

Instead, the Liberals in March 1996 reluctantly agreed that a parliamentary committee hearing should be held into the issue of sedition. Then in June 1996 the Liberals joined with the separatists to end the committee hearing. Why?

"The Reform members of the committee wanted to call top defence officials to testify but Liberal and Bloc MPs said they've had enough of Reform's attempt to paint Jean-Marc Jacob's statement as seditious," said the Canadian Press story. "Liberal MP Peter Milliken dismissed Jacob's letter—sent to military bases in Quebec days before the Oct. 30 vote—as 'material from the lunatic fringe.'

"Bloc MP Michel Bellehumeur said he deplored the Liberals taking three months to arrive at this conclusion. The Reform Party wants the committee, at the very least, to draw up guidelines for MPs when they are dealing with the military in any subsequent referendum on Quebec independence."

Fortunately, two days later the RCMP officer investigating Bouchard and Jacob for sedition under the Criminal Code personally called me to inform me that his investigation was still under way. We can still hope that charges will ultimately be laid.

Equally serious is the proof of electoral mischief. Ottawa, the Quebec Liberals, and the blue ribbon No Committee members cannot demand a recount; only the losing side could. But in light of revelations, Ottawa must establish a royal commission into massive voter disenfranchisement and voter fraud, insisting that independently appointed forensic experts be let loose to determine how widespread and concerted the electoral fraud was.

The Royal Canadian Mounted Police should have been interrogating and investigating former FLQ terrorists like Raymond Villeneuve and others for masterminding what appeared to be an orchestrated post-referendum strategy of intimidation and threats. Ottawa's health, education, and welfare authorities should have undertaken and corrected the discriminatory cost-cutting that had impaired anglophone institutions.

The federal government and people of English Canada, both inside and outside Quebec, should now do things differently. It must be made very clear to Lucien Bouchard and his separatists what will, and won't, be tolerated in future. The separatists should be put on notice that any laws that further discriminate against minorities will be disallowed. There should be no concessions or special privileges extended to Quebec, especially in the next constitutional round in 1997. Canada must reject all attempts to pander to the separatists through "distinct-society" status or other concessions such as nonsensical high-speed rail links between Toronto and Montreal. English Canadians and French Canadians are both distinct societies and no one group should enjoy more rights and privileges than the other. Any threats by Bouchard to boycott the next constitutional round, to stage another referendum, or to leave Confederation must be ignored, ridiculed, and struck down in the courts.

Some would argue that such tough-mindedness would help the separatists fan the flames among francophones in Quebec and might lead to violence. But former separatist Guy Bertrand believes that there is no massive grassroots support for outright secession among francophones. As evidence of this lack of support, Bertrand pointed out that there have never been huge mass rallies by francophones demanding independence, nor has there been large-scale support for terrorism or acts of violent defiance. Quebec journalist Benoit Aubin feels the same, arguing that the whole matter has been concocted by members of the French political and media classes, both in Quebec and in Ottawa.

In further support of their belief that mismanagement by Quebec federalists is the only problem, consider the fact that after the 1980 referendum the Parti Québécois all but abandoned the cause after Trudeau stared them down in a referendum. It was only when the Mulroney government reopened the old wounds, at the urging of his separatist supporters, that the separatists were given a chance to resurrect their crisis.

Others fear a repeat of the October Crisis of 1970, when loonies like Villeneuve and other former FLQ terrorists caused murder and mayhem. That series of incidents was not a broadly based or large uprising, but the work of a handful of violent extremists. That is interesting to note, because some francophones may think they had more reason then than now to support radical action, because anglophones then were, on average, considerably more successful in economic terms. Quebecers, like Canadians in general, are not violent people. But even if Villeneuve or others resurrect such terrorism, it is irrelevant to the tough medicine that I and others, like Bertrand, prescribe. A nation cannot govern out of fear that terrorists may misbehave.

"Canada must act, not react. The separatists do not know how to play defensive, only offensive. They have no Plan B for tough talk and fighting back," Guy Bertrand told a group of eighty high-powered businessmen and lawyers in Toronto on June 7, 1996. That day, a small ad hoc group led by myself and former Montrealer and investment banker Garrett Herman hosted a fund-raising lunch to help Bertrand cover his legal bills.

Bertrand advised toughness.

"Canadians should have another referendum, and the question should be: 'Do I want to be a citizen of Canada with Quebec included as a distinct society in terms of language and culture? Answer Yes or No'," he said. "Matters such as debt, a land bridge, and partition rules must be laid out before the next referendum. If not, and unilateral independence is attempted, there will be violence."

Bertrand also suggested, as I had written before, that if another Quebec referendum is staged by the separatists, Ottawa should make it very clear that the vote will only be equivalent to a poll and will not have the force of law. The only question that will be recognized is a direct question asking Quebecers, riding by riding, if they wish to remain Canadians or wish to create a new country. Those areas that vote to leave should make a proposal for Canada's consideration.

The threshold to embark on any such negotiations will be raised from 50 plus one percent to 66 and two-thirds percent. If some areas wish to leave and all Canadians consent, then the province should be partitioned. Areas voting No, such as the aboriginal lands, Montreal, the Ottawa Valley, and the Eastern Townships, should be promised in no uncertain terms that their right to remain part of Canada will never be negotiable.

The fact of the matter is that Canada is not divided. Quebec is divided. Canada's constitution is not flawed and does not need fixing. It only needs to be upheld by Ottawa. Quebec's French Canadians are not victims of oppression. Quebec's victims are its English Canadians. Equally victimized, indirectly, is English Canada, which has paid dearly for Ottawa's mismanagement of the problem.

Canadians must seize the agenda out of the hands of the Quebec political elites, both separatist and federalist. Canadians must understand that we would be the luckiest people on the planet if the federal government called the separatists' bluff. Parizeau and Bouchard should be forced to toe the line or to leave the country. Their mean-spirited and closed-minded games of sabotage should be understood for what they really are, and condemned

"We believe the Quebec issue must be pushed to resolution. Ottawa treats it like some constitutional disease and all we can do is relieve the pain. We say Canada must be one or two countries, not one sick nation that is constantly fighting like this," said Preston Manning in an interview in May 1996.

"What's been interesting to those of us in the Reform Party is how little English Canada has to do with any of this. This is about Quebecers fighting Quebecers in a Canadian arena. It's a family feud and the rest of the country might as well not be there. We just sit back and watch them go at it in Parliament, shouting at each other. There's a whole subtext in French between the Bloc and Liberal Quebecers that's not translated, and is pretty crude. They accuse each of other of not being here or voting for that on such-and-such a date. It's amazing and we just sit back and watch it."

The vast majority of Canadians believe in the rule of law, individual rights, and protection from discrimination. Despite the referendum's close outcome, almost 90 percent of Quebecers in a newspaper poll felt that Canada was the best country in the world. Separatists do not believe in any of these important principles. They believe they know what's best for Quebecers and will never accept that their separatism, even watered-down or hidden, has been twice rejected democratically.

Canadians must now insist that their leaders fight by staring down the separatists, including those in their own political parties. Instead, the battle has been fought by a handful of loyal and courageous anglophone and francophone Canadians. They need comrades because this is war. And Canada is worth fighting for.